15.19

Location Preferences, Migration, and Regional Growth

Niles M. Hansen

The Praeger Special Studies program—utilizing the most modern and efficient book production techniques and a selective worldwide distribution network—makes available to the academic, government, and business communities significant, timely research in U.S. and international economic, social, and political development.

Location Preferences, Migration, and Regional Growth

A Study of the South and Southwest United States

PRAEGER SPECIAL STUDIES IN U.S. ECONOMIC, SOCIAL, AND POLITICAL ISSUES

Praeger Publishers   New York   Washington   London

PRAEGER PUBLISHERS
111 Fourth Avenue, New York, N.Y. 10003, U.S.A.
5, Cromwell Place, London S.W.7, England

Published in the United States of America in 1973
by Praeger Publishers, Inc.

Library of Congress Catalog Card Number: 72-76449

Printed in the United States of America

This study may be considered as the last of three related works concerned with the integration of manpower and regional development policies. Rural Poverty and the Urban Crisis (Indiana University Press, 1970) argued that public policy should give greater emphasis to human resource investment in lagging regions and that development policy focused on places should be oriented more toward intermediate-sized growth centers. It also was proposed that comprehensive relocation assistance should be made available to residents of lagging areas who prefer to take advantage of economic opportunities in such centers. Intermediate-Size Cities as Growth Centers (Praeger Publishers, 1971) presented detailed analyses of growth-center theory and growth-center policies in the United States and abroad. It also developed criteria for growth-center policy revision, and devoted considerable attention to case studies of growth centers with relevance to lagging regions of the United States.

The present volume focuses on the location preferences of people in lagging regions under a variety of assumptions, as well as on their responsiveness to economic incentives, their expectations concerning future residential location, and actual migration patterns from lagging areas to metropolitan areas. The implications of the findings are consistent with the proposals made in the earlier studies, at least insofar as measures to influence the distribution of population and economic activity take account of the preferences of the target population.

I am grateful to the Office of Economic Research, Economic Development Administration, U.S. Department of Commerce for the financial assistance that made this study possible. William Gruben, Richard YuKhin, and Steve McNichols gave invaluable assistance in helping to collect the data for the location preference studies. Carol Pfrommer

v

.48442

provided useful criticism of the initial draft and N. Dann Milne once again gave generously of his time in the arduous task of programming and data processing in all phases of the study. David Hirschberg was also generous in lending his expertise on the Social Security sample data. Of course, without the cooperation of many persons in the survey areas, it would have been impossible to carry out this project; that they are too numerous to mention individually is another testament to the collective effort it represents. Finally I am indebted to Sandy Hooper for the high quality of the secretarial and administrative support that she lent to this entire effort.

I wish to thank a number of sources for permission to use materials published elsewhere. Part of Chapter 1 appeared in Growth and Change, II, 2 (April 1971). A portion of Chapter 2 will appear in a volume to be published under the auspices of the Commission on Population Growth and the American Future. The material on the first of the case studies discussed in Chapter 4 originally appeared in Journal of Human Resources, V, 3 (Summer 1970); the material on the Mexican Americans was published in the Social Science Quarterly, LII, 1 (June 1971). Chapter 5 is a revision of an article published in the Southern Economic Journal, XXXVIII, 4 (April 1972).

The introductory chapter presents the broad national setting for the subsequent chapters. Chapter 2 discusses the rationale for a national comprehensive relocation assistance program, while the following chapter discusses the nature and significance of location preference studies. The results of location preference studies among young persons in eastern Kentucky, south Texas, southwestern Indian reservations, and southwest Mississippi are reported in Chapter 4. Chapter 5 analyzes actual migration patterns from lagging regions to metropolitan areas. Chapter 6 gives a concluding perspective on the foregoing sections of the book.

CONTENTS

Page

PREFACE   v

LIST OF TABLES   x

Chapter

1   PROBLEMS OF DEVELOPING SMALL TOWNS
      AND LAGGING RURAL AREAS   3

      Introduction   3
      Toward a National Urban Policy   5
      National Goals and Spatial Resource
        Allocation   8
      Growth Centers, Spread Effects, and
        Rural Development   15
          Rural Industrialization and
            Return Migration: A Case
            Study of the Big Sandy Region   22
      Summary and Conclusions   28

2   THE CASE FOR ASSISTED MIGRATION   30

      Introduction   30
      The European Experience   32
      The United States Experience   39
      Implementing and Delivering Worker
        Relocation Services   54
      Summary and Conclusions   62

3   LOCATION PREFERENCE STUDIES--THEIR
      NATURE, SIGNIFICANCE, AND LIMITATIONS   64

      Introduction   64
      Residential Preferences in France   65
      Residential Preferences in the
        United States   72

The Present Studies: The Conceptual
    Rationale   77
The Present Studies: The People and
    Places   83

4   THE CASE STUDIES   93

    Introduction   93
    Eastern Kentucky--1969   94
    The Mexican Americans   100
    The Indians   111
    Southwest Mississippi   120
    Eastern Kentucky--1971   125
    Summary   130

5   MIGRATION CENTERS, GROWTH CENTERS,
    AND THE REGIONAL COMMISSIONS: AN
    ANALYSIS OF EXPECTED FUTURE LIFETIME
    INCOME GAINS TO MIGRANTS FROM
    LAGGING REGIONS   134

    Introduction   134
    The Migration Data   136
        Migrants' Expected Future Life-
            time Income Increase in
            Relation to Size of SMSA (M_{AB}):
            The Computation Process   137
        The M_{AB} Rankings   141
    Migration Centers as Growth Centers   145
    Spatial Distribution of Migration
        Centers   146
    Summary and Policy Implications   149

6   A CONCLUDING PERSPECTIVE   152

    Rural Poverty   154
    Urban Alternatives to Rural Poverty   159

Appendix

A   SINGLE DEVELOPMENT CENTER ECONOMIC
    DEVELOPMENT DISTRICTS   170

Appendix   Page

B   MULTIPLE DEVELOPMENT CENTER ECONOMIC
        DEVELOPMENT DISTRICTS   171

C   ESTIMATED MIGRATION FROM THE FOUR
        SURVEY AREAS TO SMSAs, 1965-70,
        BASED ON ONE-PERCENT SOCIAL
        SECURITY SAMPLE DATA   172

NOTES   177

ABOUT THE AUTHOR   187

LIST OF TABLES

Table | Page

1   Correlation Matrix and Regression
    Equation, Single Development Center
    EDA Districts   19

2   Correlation Matrix and Regression
    Equation, Multiple Development Center
    EDA Districts   19

3   Correlation Matrix and Regression
    Equation, All Districts with
    Development Centers   19

4   Number of Former Eastern Kentucky
    Residents Applying to American
    Standard, by State and City Size   25

5   Number of Former Eastern Kentucky
    Residents Applying to American
    Standard, by Education and City Size   27

6   Relocation Allowances in Sweden, 1958-64   37

7   Relocatees in Sweden after One Year,
    1963-64   38

8   Agencies Operating Labor Mobility
    Demonstration Projects and Number
    of Distinct Projects, by Type of
    Agency, Funding Year, and Project
    Population   40

9   Total Relocations by Type of Agency,
    Funding Year, and Project Population   42

10 Education Level of Relocatees, 1966-67
    Projects   44

11 Employment Status of Relocatees before
    Moving, 1966-67 Projects   45

12 Reasons for Moving, 1966-67 Projects   45

Table   Page

13   MDTA Training and Job Placement of
         Applicants Accepting Job Referral,
         1966-67 Projects   47

14   Relocatees Expressing Significant
         Problems with Moving, 1966-67 Projects   47

15   Starting Hourly Wages of Relocatees,
         1966-67 Projects   49

16   Importance of Relocation Allowances to
         Relocatees, 1966-67 Projects   49

17   Importance Attached by Frenchmen to
         Questions of Population, 1965   67

18   Preferred Place of Residence by Actual
         Place of Residence, France, 1965   69

19   Gallup Poll Results of Residential
         Preferences of Americans, by Selected
         Groups, February 1970   73

20   Location Preferences as Expressed in
         Pre-Relocation Interviews, 1966-67
         Labor Mobility Projects   76

21   Percentage of Pilot Demonstration
         Project Relocatees Reporting Improved
         Housing, Community Facilities, and
         Transportation, by City Size   77

22   Estimates of Components of Change for
         the Total Population and for Negroes,
         1960 to 1970, in Amite, Jefferson,
         Pike, and Walthall Counties,
         Mississippi   91

23   Relative Frequency of Location Pref-
         erences of Eastern Kentucky High
         School Seniors for Eastern Kentucky,
         Lexington or Louisville, and a
         Northern City, by Selected Groups,
         1969   95

xi

Table   Page

24   Regressions Relating Opportunity Cost
      (X) to Percentage of Students, by
      Selected Groups, Preferring a Given
      Location (Y), 1969   97

25   Expected Place of Residence in Five
      Years of Eastern Kentucky High School
      Seniors, by Sex and by College- and
      Noncollege-Bound Groups, 1969   99

26   Relative Frequency of Location Prefer-
      ences of Mexican Americans in South
      Texas for South Texas, San Antonio
      or Corpus Christi, and Dallas or
      Houston, by Selected Groups   101

27   Relative Frequency of Location Prefer-
      ences of Mexican Americans in South
      Texas for South Texas, San Antonio
      or Corpus Christi, and Chicago or
      Detroit, by Selected Groups   104

28   Relative Frequency of Location Prefer-
      ences of Mexican Americans in South
      Texas for South Texas, San Antonio
      or Corpus Christi, and Dallas or
      Houston, by Selected Groups--If
      there were a Government Relocation
      Aid Program   106

29   Relative Frequency of Location Prefer-
      ences of Mexican Americans in South
      Texas for South Texas, San Antonio
      or Corpus Christi, and Chicago or
      Detroit, by Selected Groups--If
      there were a Government Relocation
      Aid Program   107

30   Expected Place of Residence in Five
      Years: Mexican Americans in South
      Texas, by Selected Groups   108

xii

Table   Page

31   Regressions Relating Opportunity Cost
       (X) to Percentage of Respondents
       Preferring to Remain in South
       Texas (Y), by Selected Groups   109

32   Relative Frequency of Location Prefer-
       ences of New Mexico and Arizona
       Indian High School Seniors for
       their Present Community, Albuquerque,
       and Chicago, Los Angeles, or the San
       Francisco Bay Area, under Differing
       Wage Structure Assumptions   112

33   Relative Frequency of Location Prefer-
       ences of New Mexico and Arizona
       Indian High School Seniors for
       their Present Community, Albuquerque,
       and Denver, under Differing Wage
       Structure Assumptions   115

34   Expected Place of Residence in Five
       Years of New Mexico and Arizona
       Indian High School Seniors   117

35   Regressions Relating Opportunity Cost
       (X) to Percentage of Respondents
       Preferring to Remain in their
       Present Community (Y)   118

36   Relative Frequency of Location Prefer-
       ences of Southwest Mississippi Young
       People for their Present Community,
       for Jackson, Memphis, or Baton Rouge,
       and for Chicago, Detroit, Los Angeles,
       or Houston, by Selected Groups   121

37   Relative Frequency of Location Prefer-
       ences of Southwest Mississippi Young
       People, if there were a Government
       Relocation Assistance Program, by
       Selected Groups   122

38   Expected Place of Residence in Five
        Years of Southwest Mississippi
        Respondents, by Selected Groups   124

39   Regressions Relating Opportunity Cost
        (X) to Percentage of Students Pre-
        ferring to Remain in Southwest
        Mississippi (Y)   126

40   Relative Frequency of Location Prefer-
        ences of Eastern Kentucky High School
        Seniors, by Selected Groups, 1971   127

41   Relative Frequency of Location Prefer-
        ences of Eastern Kentucky High School
        Seniors, if there were a Government
        Relocation Assistance Program, by
        Selected Groups, 1971   129

42   Regressions Relating Opportunity Cost
        (X) to Percentage of Students Pre-
        ferring to Remain in Eastern
        Kentucky (Y), 1971   131

43   Expected Place of Residence in Five
        Years of Eastern Kentucky Seniors,
        by Selected Groups, 1971   131

44   Relative Frequency of Preferences for
        Home Areas, Intermediate Centers,
        and Large Cities, by Selected Groups
        of Young Persons   132

45   Age-Income Indexes (a_1), by Sex   138

46   M_{AB} Rankings of Migration Centers,
        by Regional Commission Areas   142

47   Frequency Distribution of Migration
        Centers, by Population Size, 1970   144

Table   Page

48   Number of Migration Centers Growing
      Faster than the National Average,
      1960-70, among the Fifteen and
      Five Highest-Ranking Migration
      Centers for Regional Commission
      Areas   146

49   SMSAs and Migration Centers in Regional
      Commission and Nonregional Commission
      Areas of Relevant States   147

50   Persons by Poverty Status, by Type of
      Residence, 1969   155

Location Preferences, Migration, and Regional Growth

1

PROBLEMS OF DEVELOPING SMALL TOWNS AND LAGGING RURAL AREAS

INTRODUCTION

This book deals primarily with the location preferences of young people in lagging rural areas and with actual patterns of migration from lagging regions. While these concerns may be of interest in themselves, the general aim is rather to relate them to the broader problem of the formulation of a national urban--or rural-urban--growth policy. Because this study is a direct outgrowth of several earlier works, it is in order at the outset to briefly outline this background.

In previous investigations of regional development policy in Europe and the United States, the author has applied a model relating regional development to public and private investment decisions.[1] The model distinguishes among three types of regions: congested, intermediate, and lagging. Congested regions are urban areas where the marginal net social product of further expansion would be greater in an alternative location; net social product refers here to all marginal benefits and costs, including externalities. Intermediate regions, on the other hand, offer significant advantages to private firms but they are not yet experiencing the external diseconomies associated with congested regions; expanded economic activity in these places would thus yield a greater marginal net social product than that obtained in congested regions. Lagging regions

present few attributes that would tend to attract
new economic activity. They generally are areas
characterized by small-scale agriculture or stagnant or declining industries.

On the basis of considerable theoretical and
empirical evidence, the author has argued that the
greatest relative needs of lagging regions are for
human resource development programs rather than for
infrastructure in the narrow sense. Regional policy in the United States has been primarily concerned with promoting economic development in lagging regions. Unfortunately these efforts have too
often been not only inefficient but ineffective.
From a national viewpoint it might be more efficient
to give more emphasis to human resource development
and the promotion of labor mobility than is now the
case in the mix of public policies affecting spatial resource allocation. Migrants from lagging
areas should be discouraged--or at least not en-
couraged--to move to congested regions. However,
relocation aid coupled with a program of development assistance to intermediate receiving centers
that have promising growth prospects would be an
efficient alternative. In other words, if a federal
subsidy can accelerate growth in a center that is
already growing, and if this subsidy is made condi-
tional on providing employment opportunities for
residents of lagging areas, then it could well be
more efficient to tie into the growing environment
than to attempt to create growth in a relatively
stagnant area. Of course the feasibility of this
approach depends in part on the location preferences
of people in lagging areas. Are there a significant
number of people in these places who want to move?
If so, under what conditions and to what kinds of
places do they want to move?

Since there is no question of relocating entire populations from lagging areas (i.e., we are
dealing in marginal terms), the location preference
case studies concentrate on high school seniors.
These people have relatively high mobility potential and they represent the future leadership of
the lagging areas in which they live. Moreover
they are at a stage in life when they must give at

least relatively thoughtful consideration to various employment, educational, and residential alternatives.

The significance of the location preference
studies depends on how they relate to present patterns of spatial resource allocation and to policies that are being implemented--or else considered
--to change present patterns. Thus before considering the studies in more detail it is necessary to
examine the principal efforts being made in this
regard; these are for the most part related to attempts to develop a national urban growth policy.

TOWARD A NATIONAL URBAN POLICY

In a review of recent legislation concerning a
national urban growth policy, Norman Beckman points
out

> that significant action has taken
> place--action that collectively con-
> stitutes the beginning of a reason-
> ably consistent and coherent urban
> growth policy. The evidence accumu-
> lates that the federal government and
> a significant number of states are
> coming to grips with the responsibil-
> ity to find effective ways of guiding
> and directing the inevitable growth
> and development that will occur during
> the next years.[2]

For example, the Housing and Urban Development Act
of 1970 declared that urban growth policy should:
(1) favor patterns of urbanization and economic development and stabilization that offer a range of
alternative locations and encourage the wise and
balanced use of physical and human resources in
metropolitan and urban regions, as well as in
smaller urban places with potential for accelerated
growth; (2) promote the continued economic strength
of all parts of the United States, including central cities, suburbs, smaller communities, local

neighborhoods, and rural areas; (3) help reverse
trends of migration and physical growth that reinforce disparities among states, regions, and cities;
(4) treat comprehensively the problems of poverty
and employment associated with disorderly urbanization and rural decline; (5) develop means to encourage good housing for all Americans; (6) refine
the role of the federal government in revitalizing
existing communities and encouraging planned, large-
scale urban and new community development; (7)
strengthen the capacity of general governmental institutions to contribute to balanced urban growth
and stabilization; and (8) facilitate increased coordination in the administration of federal programs to encourage desirable patterns of urban
growth and stabilization, the prudent use of natural sources, and the protection of the physical
environment.[3]

The act provides for submission by the President to Congress of a biennial report on urban
growth. The report is intended to assist in the
development of national urban growth policy and to
include information and statistics relevant to urban
growth. It would also contain a discussion of urban
problems and efforts being made at all levels of
government to deal with them, as well as recommendations for programs related to national urban policy. Finally the act also authorizes planning
grants, at three-fourths of the cost of the planning, to agencies capable of formulating plans for
determining where growth should take place in
states, regions, and smaller areas.[4]

While the Housing and Urban Development Act
urges the economic strengthening of all parts of
the country and the adoption of measures to reverse
migrations trends, the Agricultural Act of 1970
sets forth the first steps of a plan to achieve
rural development. Title 9 of the Agricultural Act
commits Congress to a policy of rural-urban balance
in the provision of government services and calls
for a series of reports on programs for rural development. Moreover federal agencies are to set up
procedures for locating new facilities in areas of
lower population density. The Department of Housing

and Urban Development and the Department of Agriculture are jointly to prepare a report to Congress
on their mutual planning efforts for rural multicounty areas outside of depressed regions.[5] The
latter regions, of course, continue to receive substantial aid from the Economic Development Administration and the regional commissions created under
the Public Works and Economic Development Act of
1965 and the Appalachian Regional Development Act
of 1965, as well as from other federal programs.

     Concern over questions of population growth
and distribution has been similarly evident in the
establishment by Congress of a Commission on Population Growth and the American Future. The commission was established to conduct and sponsor studies
and to make recommendations that may be necessary
to provide information and education on a broad
range of problems associated with the nation's population growth. The commission was instructed to
conduct inquiries into: (1) the probable course of
population growth, internal migration, and related
demographic developments between now and the year
2000; (2) the resources of the public sector of the
economy that will be required to deal with the an-
ticipated growth in population; (3) the ways in
which population growth may affect the activities
of federal, state, and local government; (4) the
impact of population growth on environmental pollution and on the depletion of natural resources; and
(5) the various means appropriate to the ethical
values and principles of society by which the nation can achieve a population level suited to its
environmental, natural resource, and other needs.[6]
At this writing, the commission is examining the
impact of rural-urban migration on those who stay
behind and on the communities in which they live.
It is also evaluating the advantages and disadvantages to those who migrate to urban centers and the
extent to which rural migrants contribute to the
problems of urban areas.

     Even before the Commission on Population
Growth and the American Future was beginning to
pose questions within the context of its mandate,
the President's National Goals Research Staff issued

a report intended to "assemble data that can help
illumine the possible range of national goals for
1976--our two hundredth anniversary . . . setting
forth some of the key choices open to us, and examining the consequences of those choices."[7]

Because the portions of this book dealing with
problems of spatial resource allocation closely reflect so many official attitudes it is necessary to
consider such allocation in some detail.

NATIONAL GOALS AND SPATIAL RESOURCE ALLOCATION

The report of the President's National Goals
Research Staff (NGRS) neither sets specific goals
with respect to urban or regional policy nor pro-
poses any plans. Rather it presents a number of
options that purport to serve as aids to relevant
public and private decision-making.

The report's concern with the regional distribution of economic activity is reflected primarily
in the section on population growth and distribution. Indeed it is an article of faith among the
staff that economic development is a lagged function of demographic change.

> Many of our large national enter-
> prises, public and private, base
> their planning for investment and
> developmental decisions on their
> perceptions of demographic trends.
> . . . [E]ach organization . . .
> seeks to shape its investment strat-
> egies to fit what it believes to be
> the most "objective" and hence the
> most probable future development
> patterns. As these policies are
> executed, the projections are power-
> fully reinforced so as to become
> self-fulfilling. Thus, in this
> sense, and without any intention to
> be so, official demographic projec-
> tions become an implicit form of
> national policy guidance.

> This being the case, one can
> imagine a positive national develop-
> ment strategy that could operate in
> essentially the same manner, but re-
> sult in a major redirection or re-
> versal of current trends.[8]

Thus the report not only adopts a highly sim-
plistic view of the growth process but also implies
that major trends in spatial resource allocation
can be altered by merely projecting one or another
pattern to the future. Hopefully it may be assumed
that no one would naively expect just any arbitrary
set of projections to influence reality. Presumably
certain explicit policy tools would be available to
induce the changes necessary to realize the projections, but the nature and significance of these
tools is not indicated. This is no doubt partly a
consequence of the staff's reluctance to recommend
any specific set of goals to which policy tools
could be tailored.

Nevertheless the report does propose alternatives and even vaguely suggests the general nature
of a future regional policy designed to induce more
geographically balanced growth. The critical issue,
according to the report, is that "Though there is
no certainty that we face an imminent problem with
the size of the population, there may be serious
problems of over-population and under-population in
various areas of the United States. Many experts
believe that population shifts of the last two
decades have had very detrimental effects on many
rural areas, while simultaneously greatly aggravat-
ing urban problems."[9] A familiar catalogue of
urban and regional difficulties is set forth: ex-
change of rural poverty in the South for urban
slums in northern cities by migration of people
with inadequate access to human resource investments; lack of access to suburban jobs by the inner
city's poor, especially blacks; overconcentration
of population and economic activity in a few urban
regions; and heavy outmigration from many rural
areas.

The report is particularly critical of megalopolis. "The merits of sheer size," it points out,

"now appear more debatable than heretofore, particularly in the case of large metropolitan areas.
Large concentrations of population generate serious
pollution problems, traffic congestion, and higher
per capita public expenditures. And they are un-
duly vulnerable to power failures, riots, and other
disruptive social action."[10] Therefore, the report
concludes, "Apropos of population distribution, we
need to decide on whether or not we will adopt a
deliberate strategy to encourage internal migration
to negate the forecasts of ever-growing urban congestion in a few megalopoli."[11]

Three alternatives are discussed that could
foster "more balanced" national growth: (1) development of sparsely populated rural areas; (2) promotion of existing small cities and towns in nonmetropolitan areas; and (3) creation of new towns
outside of present metropolitan areas. The first
approach has been urged by numerous defenders of
rural places. The report is correct in maintaining
that this approach is rejected by most economists
and that almost every experiment of this kind has
been not only inefficient but also ineffective.
The report is rather noncommittal with respect to
new towns, though it seems to regard them more fa-
vorably for their limited experimental value than
for their feasibility as vehicles for absorbing a
major share of future national population growth.

In the most sensible article yet written on
the subject of new towns, William Alonso concludes
that "A policy of using some new towns as instru-
ments for increasing knowledge seems indicated on a
number of grounds; but it should avoid both the ex-
tremes of the mindless advocacy of diversity for
its own sake without regard to cost and expected
benefits, and the extreme of support of redundant
experiments which do not contribute to knowledge."[12]
Whether or not Alonso's reflections were available
to the NGRS is not known to this writer, but it is
well that there are indications that they were.

Without being explicit on the matter, the report seems to favor a growth-center strategy based
on "middle-sized communities (usually upwards of
50,000--but as small as 25,000) which are growing

or which have the potential for self-sustained
growth."[13] Growth centers would provide a migration alternative to the larger cities as well as
beneficial "spread effects" to their rural hinterlands. Growth centers "would provide promising opportunities for more balanced growth" by absorbing
natural increases in their own populations and rural and foreign migration that may otherwise go to
large metropolitan regions. But for a growth center policy to be effective there would need to be

> some redirection of public expendi-
> tures and new forms of partnerships
> between the public and private sec-
> tors as well as through possible ma-
> jor increases in public outlays.
> Indeed, some redirection of expendi-
> tures may be crucial to assuring that
> balanced growth will be realized,
> since otherwise we will continue to
> have vast expenditures competing for
> the realization of conflicting ob-
> jectives.[14]

More explicitly, although the report alludes
to the importance of proximity to metropolitan
areas in improving the social and economic conditions of rural areas, nothing is done with this
knowledge. From contacts that this writer had with
the National Goals Research Staff during the preparation of its report, it is apparent that the NGRS
was familiar with the research activities of the
University of Chicago's Center for Urban Studies.
Brian Berry has summarized the center's conclusions
in the following terms: "Our thesis is very simple:
the degree of metropolitan labor market participation is the key variable in the 'regional welfare
syndrome,' indexing the gradient of urban influence
on surrounding areas."[15] Mapping studies carried
out at the Center for Urban Studies demonstrated that

> Examination of the gradients of in-
> fluence of smaller centers indicates
> clearly enough that there seems little

> sense in trying to use very small ur-
> ban places as growth centers. Their
> regional influence is too limited.
> Indeed, very few cities of less than
> 40,000 to 50,000 population appear to
> have any impact on the regional wel-
> fare syndrome, although admittedly
> the few that do are located in the
> more peripheral areas.[16]

One can only speculate about the hidden agenda that
led the NGRS to ignore these findings.

Sidestepping Berry's conclusions, the NGRS approach to growth centers is not unlike the growth
center policy now being implemented by the Economic
Development Administration (EDA) under provisions
of the Public Works and Economic Development Act of
1965. These centers have tended to be quite small.
As of April 15, 1970, there were 87 EDA-designated
economic development districts with 171 development
centers (126 economic development centers and 45
redevelopment centers). Only 30 of the development
centers had populations greater than 50,000 and
only 13 had populations greater than 100,000.
Forty-two of the centers had fewer than 10,000 persons. Moreover, between 1960 and 1970, 61 percent
of the development centers that had been designated
as of April 15, 1970 had population growth below
the national average; 38 percent of the development
centers (and more than 50 percent of the redevelopment centers) experienced population declines. In
addition, as is shown later in this chapter, the
existence of beneficial spread effects from growth
centers--even when they are rapidly growing on a
de facto basis and not simply designated on political grounds--is questionable.

What is particularly perplexing about the EDA
growth-center designations is that the authorizing
legislation placed a 250,000 maximum-size limitation on growth centers. Thus the EDA growth centers could have been much larger than has actually
been the case. In this regard it is instructive to
note the conclusions drawn by participants from
many countries at a conference on regional

development problems sponsored by the International
Economic Association. In response to the question
"How large must a successful growth point be?" it
was generally held that

> the minimum size of growth points
> that experience has shown to be suc-
> cessful was nearer to a population
> of 100,000 than to one of 10,000, and
> that even 100,000 was more likely to
> be an underestimate than an overesti-
> mate. It must be large enough to pro-
> vide efficiently the main services of
> education, medical facilities, bank-
> ing, shopping facilities. . . . Above
> all, it must be large enough both to
> provide an efficient infrastructure
> of public utility services, and to
> permit the early and progressive
> growth of external economies for its
> local industry.[17]

Thus while the report dwells on the disadvantages of large size it neglects another issue of
equal interest for growth centers; namely, the viable minimum size for growth centers. What is
hazarded in this regard in the report reflects too
much optimism concerning the economic importance of
small towns. One should at least be aware of the
economic opportunities foregone in order to realize
political objectives, such as subsidizing places
for their own sake.

Related to the report's small-town bias is its
concern for areas of the country experiencing outmigration. But it is one thing to be perturbed
about the transfer of rural poverty to urban ghettos
and quite another to worry about population declines
in rural areas of Missouri, Kansas, Nebraska, Illi-
nois, and the Dakotas. The fact that increasingly
efficient agriculture does not require as many farm
workers as before, and will need still fewer in the
future, does not mean that we are dealing with
problems related to low income and high unemployment. While it may be true that some of those left

behind in these areas are experiencing the unfortunate effects of stagnation and lack of economic opportunity, the problem is essentially one of ad-
justing to success. The greatest acceleration in
the growth rate of nonmetropolitan income has been
in the Plains,* rising from a rate of change of 2.9
percent during the 1950s to 6.2 percent in the
1960s.[18] In contrast is the situation in much of
the South and other areas where neglect of human
resources constitutes a national scandal.

Perhaps the basic problem with the report, in
the present context, is its failure to specify in
more concrete terms what it means by "balanced
growth." Should equality of per capita income,
public overhead capital, education and health, or
economic activity (however defined) be a national
goal? Should the growth of lagging areas be promoted solely by moving resources to them and by
creating new resources within their boundaries, or
should we give more attention to comprehensive relocation assistance programs? What effects would
the induced location of economic activity in a given
region have on other regions? How could conflicts
between attempts to maximize regional and national
welfare be resolved or at least ameliorated? Until
we are able to answer questions of this nature, it
is not operationally feasible to appeal to "balanced growth."

To be sure, the report is in many respects an
improvement on The People Left Behind,[19] Communities of Tomorrow,[20] and similar documents that have
advocated, at least by implication, public policy
measures that would swim against the urbanization
stream. If the nation's biggest urban complexes
are overcrowded, this does not necessarily imply a
need for policies to force-feed growth in lagging,
and for the most part rural, areas. There are numerous intermediate-sized cities that may serve as

-----

*For our purposes, the "Plains" include the
states of Minnesota, Iowa, Missouri, North Dakota,
South Dakota, Nebraska, and Kansas.

growth centers benefiting people from lagging areas.
Policies related to these areas and measures to
provide relocation assistance on a voluntary basis
represent the most conspicuous gaps in the nation's
regional and urban policy mix. The report hints at
these alternatives, but too frequently it turns
vague and timid just when it seems ready to come to
grips with important problems. Indeed it is often
cautious to the point of blandness. In consequence
its impact unfortunately will probably not be com-
mensurate with the work that went into it. While
it raises important issues, its failure to take a
stand represents a lost opportunity to provoke the
kind of public debate required if good ideas are to
be implemented in the legislative process.

GROWTH CENTERS, SPREAD EFFECTS,
AND RURAL DEVELOPMENT

Considerable importance has been attached,
both in the United States and abroad, to growth-
center strategies for the development of lagging
and primarily rural areas. It is therefore instructive to consider empirical evidence concerning
their principal rationale; namely, the generation
of spread effects that are supposed to benefit the
hinterlands. This section examines the evidence
for the only growth-center strategy influential on
a national scale in the United States, that of the
Economic Development Administration.

The Public Works and Economic Development Act
of 1965 created the Economic Development Administration and directed it to administer grants and
loans for public works and development facilities,
industrial and commercial loans and loan guarantees,
and an extensive planning, research,and technical
assistance program to assist the development of
economically lagging areas. To facilitate efficient and effective economic development planning,
EDA encourages counties with high unemployment
and/or low income--termed redevelopment areas--to
form multi-county economic development districts.
Each of these districts is required to designate at

least one growth center. A growth center is expected to have the "potential to stimulate the economic growth of the district so that its economic
growth may reasonably be expected to contribute to
to the alleviation of distress"[21] in the remaining
areas of the district.

EDA's growth-center strategy is based on the
premise that the growth center will diffuse growth
to its hinterland. This critical assumption is
also made in a great deal of the relevant scholarly
literature. In a recent article for example, a
growth center was defined as "an urban centre of
economic activity which can achieve self-sustaining
growth to the point that growth is diffused outward
into the pole region and eventually into the less
developed region of the nation."[22]

Perroux's classic article on growth poles argues that "growth does not appear everywhere and
all at once; it appears in points or development
poles, with variable intensities; it spreads along
diverse channels and with varying terminal effects
for the whole economy."[23] These growth poles are
assumed by Boudeville to be composed of a complex
of propulsive industries. A propulsive industry
has two characteristics: (1) a direct and indirect
dominating influence over all other activities, and
(2) an oligopolistic concentration of firms with
price leadership. Growth is assumed to be transmitted via the interindustry linkages of the propulsive industries.[24] Although the orthodox Perroux
thesis limits the analysis of these ties to sectoral
relationships in economic space, it may be inferred
that the growth pole could diffuse growth to its
hinterland through interactions between the propulsive industries located in the growth pole and satellite industries located in the hinterland.

A similar thesis has been expounded by Hirschman,[25] who has analyzed regional transmission of
growth in terms of a dichotomy between advanced and
backward areas. The advanced areas are spontane-
ously growing and possess characteristics generally
associated with growth centers, such as abundant
infrastructure, economies of scale, and agglomera-
tion economies. In assessing the role of growth

centers in promoting regional development, Hirschman holds that "once growth takes a firm hold in one part of the national territory, it obviously sets in motion certain forces that act on the remaining parts."[26] This alleged diffusion of growth is assumed to be facilitated by increased investments and purchases by the growth center in the backward area via interindustry linkages between the key industries in the growth center and the satellite industries in the backward area. Hirschman also counts on political forces to help redress disparities between growth centers and lagging areas.

Despite these and related efforts to develop a rationale for the growth transmission phenomenon of growth centers, there has been a remarkable lack of studies on whether the growth of growth centers does in fact spread to their hinterlands. However my colleague Richard YuKhin has made a noteworthy effort in this regard. He employed multiple regression analyses to examine economic relationships between EDA growth centers and their respective hinterlands. Four independent variables were used: (1) growth center's personal income growth rate, 1959-68; (2) growth center's personal income growth rate, 1950-59 (a lagged variable); (3) population size of the growth center (growth diffusion is assumed to be a function of size by Berry and others[27]); and (4) ratio of growth center to hinterland population. These were regressed against the dependent variable, the hinterland's personal income growth rate (1959-68). The data were compiled from the Regional Economic Information System of the Office of Business Economics (of the Department of Commerce). Per capita variables were not employed in the analysis because of inaccurate population estimates in the regional system for the period in question. Data were available for 77 economic development districts designated by the Economic Development Administration as of April 15, 1970, but the scope of YuKhin's study was limited to the 64 "development centers" because the 13 "redevelopment centers" were not regarded as growth centers by EDA.

Data for the independent and dependent variables are shown in Appendixes A and B. Data for
the development districts with single growth centers are shown in Appendix A. Data for the development districts with multiple growth centers are
shown in Appendix B. In this group the growth center with the highest population growth rate during
the 1960-70 period was selected, except in cases
where the largest growth center was over twice as
large as the next largest center. In such cases
the largest center was treated as the growth center
and the remaining areas in the development district
were treated as the hinterland. In both Appendix A
and Appendix B, redevelopment centers were treated
as part of the hinterland. These procedures were
adopted after consultation with EDA personnel familiar with the data.

Multiple regression equations were calculated
for 30 single growth-center development districts,
34 multiple growth-center development districts;
and all 64 development districts. Table 1 shows
the correlation matrix as well as the regression
equation for single development center EDA districts.
In the table, Y equals personal income growth rate
(1959-68) in the hinterland; X equals growth center's personal income growth rate, 1959-68; X_2 equals
growth center's personal income growth rate, 1950-59;
X_3 equals population size of the growth center; and
X_4 equals population ratio of growth center to hinterland. The values in parentheses are the t-values.
Only X_1 is significant at the .05 level, though it
is not significant at the .01 level. The R^2 value
is .22, insignificant at the .05 level.

Table 2 shows the correlation matrix and regression equation for multiple development center
EDA districts. X_1 and X_2 are both significant at
the .05 level, though neither is significant at the
.01 level. The R^2 value, .26, is not significant
at the .05 level.

Table 3 shows the correlation matrix and regression equation for all economic development centers in EDA districts. X_1 is significant at the
.01 level and X_2 at the .05 level. The R^2 value is
.20, insignificant at the .05 level.

TABLE 1

Correlation Matrix and Regression Equation,
Single Development Center EDA Districts

	X_1	X_2	X_3	X_4
X_2	.09694			
X_3	-.31004	.22029		
X_4	-.32182	.05086	.80436	
Y	.31004	.26441	.20261	.13332

$$Y = 14.28 + .487X_1 + .237X_2 + .0015X_3 + .00091X_4$$
$$\quad\quad\quad (2.035) \quad (0.9136) \quad (0.7596) \quad (0.1847)$$

TABLE 2

Correlation Matrix and Regression Equation,
Multiple Development Center EDA Districts

	X_1	X_2	X_3	X_4
X_2	.10276			
X_3	-.05730	.10349		
X_4	.03064	.10897	.73663	
Y	.44007	.34948	-.07078	.07055

$$Y = 49.7 + .306X_1 + .166X_2 + .000068X_3 + .000369X_4$$
$$\quad\quad\quad (2.578) \quad (2.062) \quad (-0.9708) \quad (0.8271)$$

TABLE 3

Correlation Matrix and Regression Equation,
All Districts with Development Centers

	X_1	X_2	X_3	X_4
X_2	.10205			
X_3	-.14500	.14089		
X_4	-.00800	.10736	.67886	
Y	.36192	.29120	.06972	.07217

$$Y = 36.8 + 0.36X_1 + 0.1957X_2 + .000442X_3 - .000613X_4$$
$$\quad\quad\quad (2.945) \quad (2.057) \quad (.6081) \quad (-0.1137)$$

These results do not permit firm generalizations about the presence of spread effects. The
significant regression coefficients are particularly
noteworthy because the dependent variable and the
relevant independent variables all consist of rates
of change, and close relationships are not easily
come by in such cases. On the other hand, none of
the R^2 values is significant. Also, association
between growth in the hinterlands and growth in the
development centers does not imply that all growth
centers are performing well in terms of increasing
incomes. Twenty-eight of the development centers
and 25 of the hinterland areas had 1959-68 personal
income growth below the national rate of 78.6 percent. Moreover, given the nature of the regions in
question, for the most part they started from a
relatively low 1959 base.

It should also be pointed out that a more comprehensive analysis of the nature of spread effects
would have to take account of such variables as migration, commuting, natural population increase,
and specifically regional influences that may be
operating. In the absence of such studies, it may
be tentatively concluded that the results of YuKhin's
work are consistent with other findings indicating
that spread effects from induced growth centers are
likely to be nonexistent[28] or at best ambiguous.[29]

In any case it must be recognized that unless
the quality of human resources is improved in lagging regions there will continue to be severe problems of adjustment to rural-urban migration as well
as a regional labor supply attractive only to firms
seeking a cheap and hopefully nonunion work force.
For example a recent study of the degree to which
industrialization in the Ozarks region has bypassed
the rural poor concludes that "inmigrants tended to
intervene between jobs and the rural poor who would
be targets for an industrialization program."[30] It
was found that

> Many families accepted lower incomes
> when they moved into the Ozarks, and
> in effect, moved into poverty. These
> groups contributed a further complica-
> tion to the poverty problem.

> The evidence of this study is
> conclusive that the job leakage to
> inmigrants is great enough to war-
> rant serious consideration. Addi-
> tional evidence should be welcomed
> by policy makers who are searching
> for more efficient approaches to the
> problem. Industrialization can be a
> major component of a poverty policy,
> but from the perspective of the un-
> skilled rural poor in the Ozarks,
> the strength of the approach needs
> to be improved with auxiliary
> measures.[31]

Similarly Irwin Gray undertook a case study
of the employment effects of a new industry in rural West Virginia. After building a major aluminum
reduction and rolling mill at Ravenswood, Kaiser
Aluminum and Chemical Corporation attempted to hire
as many workers as possible from the local areas.
But it soon became clear that directly applicable
skills and even basic adequate schooling were lacking in the local manpower pool. The kind of worker
needed by Kaiser was likely to be a person already
employed, a migrant from the region who now desired
to return, or a person on temporary layoff from
some other plant in the Ohio valley. The direct
effects from the standpoint of lesser-qualified
persons seeking employment were disappointing.
Perhaps 300 jobs were created locally as a result
of Ravenswood's growth, but they were primarily in
low-skill retail trade employment. New professional
openings were filled almost exclusively by persons
from outside the community. Lack of capital and of
local entrepreneurship prevented local people from
establishing new businesses. In general, Gray concludes that "more local people could be at work, at
the expense of in-migrants, if they had had the
necessary minimum education or training. . . . That
more were not hired brings up some pointed questions
about education and skills in general."[32]
Another central Appalachian area, the Big Sandy
region of eastern Kentucky, where two of the location preference studies discussed in Chapter 4 were

made, also provides relevant insights into the return migration phenomenon.

Rural Industrialization and Return Migration: A Case Study of the Big Sandy Region

The Big Sandy Development District, in the heart of central Appalachia,* comprising a five-county area, is one of the poorest areas in the United States: its 1966 unemployment rate was 14.7 percent; its per capita income in 1963 was only $1,025, compared to $1,799 for all of Kentucky and $2,488 for the United States; its infant mortality rate of 28.0 per thousand live births in 1966 was higher than the national rate of 25.1; and, according to the 1960 Census of Housing, only 56 percent of its housing units were of sound structure. In 1965 the Kentucky superintendent of public instruction estimated that 418 additional classrooms were needed in the Big Sandy.[33] Between 1960 and 1970, while the nation's population was growing by over 31 percent, all five of the Big Sandy counties declined absolutely and three of them lost over 10 percent of their population.[34]

Despite the Big Sandy's problems, it has received considerable attention as a model for cooperative local development efforts. The city of Pikeville, which was named an All America City in 1966, and the cooperative efforts of Pikeville, Paintsville, and Prestonsburg, were the subjects of feature articles in Appalachia, the Journal of the Appalachian Regional Commission (ARC), in 1969.[35] The commission, along with the Economic Development Administration and the Kentucky Program Development Office, has promoted cooperation among the county and city governments of the Big Sandy in placing investments where they will most benefit the entire area. After reviewing some of the projects that

---

*The Big Sandy counties are Floyd, Johnson, Magoffin, Martin, and Pike.

have recently been initiated in the area, the commission's journal concluded that "all improvements
in the three cities and in the entire valley have
occurred within a framework of development district
planning and organization which is virtually an action model of the Appalachian development concept."[36]

The Big Sandy's development efforts have frequently been cited in the national news media.
Business Week, for example, devoted an article to
the Appalachian program and to the Big Sandy as an
example of the positive achievements of the Appalachian Regional Commission approach to comprehensive
development planning. "Big Sandy," it remarked,
"in fact, is the ARC's idea of how a local district
ought to work."[37]

Others are more pessimistic. For example,
such critics as Luther Carter and Harry Caudill
have insisted that the Appalachian Regional Commission has been leery of pressing for either tighter
controls on strip mining or a severance, or production, tax on coal in the Big Sandy, which is a
major coal-mining area. "In sum," writes Carter,
"the Appalachian program has provided a test of a
promising new mechanism for a joint federal, state,
and local attack on regional development problems.
But, up to now, that attack has not reached to two
gut issues--issues which cannot be avoided much
longer without leaving ARC open to charges of a
shameless dereliction of duty."[38]

Similarly, a front-page review in The New York
Times of the Appalachian program found that despite
some $7 billion in public investment in Appalachia,
the poor people of eastern Kentucky and of West
Virginia have been little affected. Because of its
obvious relevance here, a part of this report
should be quoted at length:

> Some O.E.O. [Office of Economic Op-
> portunity] activists here [in eastern
> Kentucky] see the Appalachian program
> as chiefly a boon for the rich and
> for entrenched political interests.
>   To gain benefits, the isolated
> poor--a majority of the population
> here in central Appalachia--must

come out of the creeks and hollows to
revived employment centers. The
trouble is that many either won't or
can't.

A classic example is Pikeville,
Kentucky. There, in a gritty coal
town that follows a narrow strip of
river bottom flatland . . . the Federal and state governments have been
persuaded to invest $22.5 million in
the construction of a huge mountain
cut.

The vast channel will reroute a
new four-lane highway, the Chesapeake
and Ohio Railway tracks and the course
of the Big Sandy River itself away
from a congested center of about 6,000
people, thus opening 200 acres of land
to be reclaimed and developed by the
townsfolk.

Pikeville, chosen as a strategic
"growth center" for the 60,000 people
in rural Pike County, would have continued to die without this vast effort. The project is putting the
place on the map if only because the
dirt to be moved is greater than the
bulk of Grand Coulee Dam. But the
effort has generated skepticism.

Among the "generally discouraging
statistical facts" about central Appalachia . . . is the discovery that
barely 12 per cent of the total population here is living in towns.[39]

Whether the Pikeville mountain cut and the
millions of other dollars being poured into the Big
Sandy will make the area attractive to a significant amount of new economic activity still remains
to be seen. Defenders of the vast public outlays
in the area usually point to the opening of a $5
million American Standard plant as a harbinger of
things to come. The plant, virtually the first
major heavy industry location in central Appalachia,

is supposed to employ around 400 persons when in
full operation. As one observer points out, the
plant "has been hailed as a pilot project which may
be the first step in pumping new blood into the
region's economic veins. But the people it has
brought 'back home' could be the beginning of an
even more important revolution in the hills."[40]

Richard YuKhin has examined the characteristics
of potential return migrants to the Big Sandy on
the basis of 998 applications received from former
area residents by American Standard. Table 4 shows
the place of residence of the applicants by state
and the size of cities in which they resided.

TABLE 4

Number of Former Eastern Kentucky Residents
Applying to American Standard,
by State and City Size

| State | City Size | | | All Cities |
	Large	Medium	Small	
Illinois	14	2	0	16 (1.7)
Indiana	11	7	98	116 (12.0)
Kentucky	24	50	2	76 (7.9)
Michigan	114	50	17	181 (18.7)
Ohio	288	73	140	501 (51.9)
West Virginia	1	10	6	17 (1.8)
Others	18	22	19	59 (6.1)
Total	470 (48.7)	214 (22.2)	282 (29.2)	966 (100.0)

Note: Figures given in parentheses are percentages. Also, individual percentages do not add
to 100 because of rounding.

YuKhin defined a large city as one with over 500,000
residents, a medium-sized city as one with between
50,000 and 500,000, a small city as one with less
than 50,000. Nearly 50 percent of the applicants
lived in large cities; 29.2 percent lived in small
cities, and 22.2 percent lived in medium-sized
cities. A majority of the total were in Ohio.
Ninety percent of the applicants were males and
85.3 percent were employed at the time of application.

Table 5 shows the breakdown of applicants by
city size and education. Of the total, 88.5 percent
had at least a high school diploma. In addition
2.3 percent of the non-high school graduates had
completed vocational educational training. Thus a
large pool of educated people could be expected to
return to eastern Kentucky if employment were
available; this lends support to the American Standard personnel manager's assertion that "you could
man five factories like this with qualified, capable people within 30 days."[41] Moreover most of
the applicants were young, 79 percent being under
the age of 35. Thus if employment opportunities
are generated in eastern Kentucky, the return migrants are likely to be young people able to assist
in the development of the area rather than older
people nearing retirement.

The American Standard data also indicate that
potential returnees would be willing to accept wage
reductions to return to eastern Kentucky. YuKhin
compared current or last wage of applicants with
the wage they would accept to return to eastern
Kentucky. The applicants from large cities would
be willing to return to the Big Sandy region for a
weighted average of 81 percent of their current or
last wage. The comparable figures for applicants
from the medium-sized and small cities were 91 percent and 87 percent respectively. Allowing for
cost of living, one could expect applicants from
small cities to accept the smallest wage reduction.
The reasons why respondents from medium-sized cities
would accept the greatest reductions may be related
to their being relatively well assimilated in their
present communities. In any case the data indicate

TABLE 5

Number of Former Eastern Kentucky Residents Applying to
American Standard, by Education and City Size

Educational Attainment	City Size			
	Large	Medium	Small	All Cities
Eighth grade and under	7 (1.5)	4 (1.9)	15 (5.3)	26 (2.7)
Nine through twelve (did not graduate)	25 (5.3)	16 (7.6)	22 (7.8)	63 (6.5)
Nine through twelve (did not graduate) and vocational school	9 (1.9)	6 (2.8)	7 (2.5)	22 (2.3)
High school graduate	320 (68.0)	117 (55.2)	190 (67.6)	627 (65.1)
High school graduate and vocational school	51 (10.8)	25 (11.8)	14 (5.0)	90 (9.4)
Thirteen and over	45 (9.6)	35 (16.5)	23 (8.2)	103 (10.7)
Thirteen and vocational school	0	1 (0.4)	0	1 (0.7)
College graduate	13 (2.8)	8 (3.8)	10 (3.6)	31 (3.2)
Total	470 (100.0)	212 (100.0)	281 (100.0)	963 (100.0)

Note: Figures given in parentheses are percentages. Also, individual percentages do not add to 100 because of rounding.

27

that even if the local labor pool cannot satisfy
skilled manpower requirements, this need not be a
barrier to the attraction of heavy industry.

SUMMARY AND CONCLUSIONS

There is currently an unprecedented interest
in the formulation of policies to influence the
geographic distribution of population and economic
activity in the United States. Although more comprehensive approaches are now under consideration,
primary emphasis has been given to programs to promote the development of lagging, and for the most
part rural, areas. Of course not even the strongest rural development advocates would argue that
all rural areas are economically viable. Thus development legislation has stipulated that investments be made in areas with significant growth potential, on the theory that once economic expansion
is induced in these growth centers, the hinterlands
will benefit from beneficial spread effects. Unfortunately the evidence indicates that this approach has not been successful. In consequence
some critics have advocated placing more funds directly into the most distressed counties. However
such an approach seems to be nothing more than the
"worst first" policy that the Economic Development
Administration has actively considered along with
the growth-center strategy, despite the inconsis-
tency of the two approaches. To attempt to give
top priority to the least promising areas may be
justifiable in welfare terms, but it would seem to
bear little relationship to serious efforts to promote regional development.
Charles Fairchild points out that "the apparent failure of redevelopment efforts to solve the
problems of structural unemployment in depressed
regions [has] led many authorities to recommend a
program of relocation assistance to increase migration from rural areas and to direct it toward regional centers of economic growth."[42] In other
words, if the nation's biggest urban complexes are
overcrowded, this does not necessarily imply that

policies should attempt to force-feed growth in lagging rural areas. There are numerous intermediate-
sized cities that may serve as growth centers for
policy purposes, but their primary function would
be to benefit people from lagging areas as migration centers rather than as generators of spread
effects. Policies related to these areas, together
with measures to provide relocation assistance on a
voluntary basis, represent the most conspicuous
gaps in the nation's regional and urban policy mix.
While programs that would increase mobility may be
unpopular with local political leaders in lagging
areas, they could be made more acceptable by emphasizing outmigration as a human resource investment
and by emphasizing that the departure may be only
temporary, since high return migration can be expected if and when economic opportunities develop
in the lagging areas.

2

**THE CASE FOR
ASSISTED MIGRATION**

INTRODUCTION

In general, Americans are very mobile people.
One need only recall such phenomena as the great
westward expansion and the outmigration of southern
blacks to northern cities in the past several decades. Even today 20 percent of all Americans move
to a different house every year. Between 5 and 7
percent move to a different county every year; of
these half move to a different state. Over 75 percent of the people live outside of the state where
they were born.[1] If only males in the labor force
are considered, it has been estimated that about 7
percent move between counties in a year; most of
these 4.6 million intercounty movers are in the 22-
44 age group, are married, and have completed at
least 12 years of school. The highest migration
rates, however, are for men aged 22-24, unmarried,
unemployed or in the armed services, who have attended college.[2]

Most of the large number of persons in the
labor force who move every year do so primarily for
economic reasons.[3] Inmigration to receiving areas
is closely related to the attractiveness of their
labor markets to job seekers. Active demand for
labor attracts persons from both economically depressed and economically healthy areas. However,
outmigration from metropolitan areas appears to be

primarily spontaneous and not responsive to local
labor market conditions. In other words, in the
normal geographic circulation of the more mobile
elements of the population, there is as much movement from prosperous areas as from depressed areas.
But prosperous areas replace their outmigration by
attracting an even greater influx of persons from
elsewhere. The depressed area, on the other hand,
is usually not able to replace its population loss.
The weakness of its "pull" rather than the strength
of its "push" is therefore mostly responsible for
its net migration loss.[4]

In addition to the economic factor, there is a
great deal of group migration from lagging areas.
Varden Fuller points out that group migration patterns

> have been--and are still--more charac-
> teristic of the South and the southern
> Appalachian regions. The current mi-
> gration from the rural South to northern
> metropolitan centers apparently depends
> very heavily upon kin and friendship.
> This is not a new pattern for the South;
> nor is it confined to Negroes. It is
> part of a cultural pattern or group
> self-dependence in the South as against
> individualistic self-dependence in the
> North. Other group patterns that are
> partly regional and partly ethnic are
> to be found among Mexican-Americans
> and in the off-reservation movements
> of Indians. In the North and West,
> individualism seems to be otherwise
> dominant.[5]

It is particularly important to stress that
while group migration may provide a valuable framework of support to the migrant, this phenomenon is
not always consistent with economically rational
choice. Many of the persons who belong to the
groups that are the principal concern of this book

> leave only because they have no choice;
> they can't eke out a living where they

are. Among these can be found four
major categories of desperately poor
people: Southern blacks, Appalachian
whites, Mexican-Americans and American Indians.

Once they reach the city, their
situation often improves, often
doesn't, and sometimes it gets worse.
Generally these young people have made
their move with little help or information about where the decent jobs are
and little cash to tide them over until
the right one is found. Following
their relatives and old friends, they
often go to precisely the places where
an oversupply of unskilled labor already exists.[6]

The frequent lack of economic gain associated
with rural to urban migration has been noted in a
number of studies.[7] It would seem, therefore, that
a comprehensive and permanent relocation assistance
program could be of considerable value in providing
accurate labor market information and necessary supportive services. That such programs are feasible
has been demonstrated by both European and American
experience, which will now be considered in some
detail.

THE EUROPEAN EXPERIENCE

All major western European countries now have
some form of subsidy to assist persons migrating
from rural to urban areas. In general there are
nine forms of aid: (1) interregional clearing systems, (2) travel assistance, (3) financial assistance to commuters, (4) starting assistance, (5)
lodging and maintenance assistance to single people,
(6) provision of hostels, (7) separation allowances
and allowances for traveling home, (8) assistance
for removal of household, and (9) assistance for
housing and installation of family.[8]

In the case of interregional clearance systems,
job vacancies and job openings are reported to the

employment service first at the local level and
then at the district or regional level, before national clearance comes into operation. Lists of
job openings at the national level are usually com-
municated to local employment offices weekly; in
Belgium and Sweden, though, this is done daily. On
the other hand, regular lists of job seekers are
compiled and circulated only in Sweden, Norway, the
Netherlands, and West Germany. In some countries
information about job vacancies and job applications
are transmitted through the mass media. In Sweden,
employment service officers from receiving areas
are temporarily assigned to departure areas. In
West Germany and the Netherlands there are special
interregional clearance services for specific kinds
of jobs and for job applicants with high rates of
interregional mobility.

The minimum travel assistance aid--that existing in France--is an advance for travel expenses to
take up a new job; the maximum--that in Sweden and
Norway--is a travel and subsistance grant for job
seeking workers and their families. West Germany
and Belgium assist job seekers but without the worker's family. In Belgium, France, West Germany, the
Netherlands, Sweden, and the United Kingdom, travel
assistance is given for training in other areas,
while West Germany also aids travel to take job selection tests. In Denmark, assistance is limited
to travel to take up a job. Travel assistance is
given in the form of grants only in Sweden, Norway,
France, Belgium, and Denmark. The Dutch and West
German schemes also provide for loans, and the Brit-
ish one provides for advances. Commuting assistance
is given in Sweden, France, the Netherlands, Denmark, West Germany, and Belgium.

Starting assistance to cover living costs until
the first pay day is granted in Sweden, Norway, West
Germany, and the United Kingdom. This assistance is
particularly significant in Sweden and Norway. Norway pays the whole allowance immediately after relocation, while Sweden has introduced a sliding scale
according to the expected duration of employment.
If a Swedish worker terminates his employment and
returns home without good reason, he must refund the
appropriate proportion of his starting assistance.

This does not apply, however, to job changes within the receiving area, providing that they have been approved by the employment service.

Lodging and maintenance assistance for single persons in Western Europe is largely confined to trainees. With the exception of Sweden and to a certain extent the United Kingdom, these allowances are not primarily related to labor surplus problems in depressed areas. Some countries give aid for the construction of hostels for young single persons, but this assistance plays only a limited part in geographic mobility programs.

In Sweden, Norway, West Germany, and the United Kingdom, separation allowances and travel allowances to visit families are granted for certain periods to all persons living away from home. The nature of separation-from-family allowances varies greatly. Sweden takes into account the size of the family and has a limit of one year; the allowance is reduced by 25 percent each quarter. In Norway the maximum duration is 20 weeks and the rates are calculated on a monthly or daily basis. In West Germany the allowances are based on the weekly wage rate, the distance involved, and the duration of separation.

Travel allowances for visits at home with families also vary greatly. In Sweden and Norway, 100 percent of travel costs are covered, subject to the same restrictions applying to travel assistance to seek or take up jobs. Most countries, however, cover only a part of these expenses. The number of assisted visits is limited in most countries. In Sweden, for example, the number is one per month, while in the United Kingdom it is three per year for young trainees and six per year for adults.

Most countries provide for moving household effects. Payments are generally made retroactive, but often the relocated person is not required to advance all the costs. The usual form of assistance is a grant, although in West Germany loans are also made. With the exception of Norway, which reimburses 75 percent of moving costs, most countries reimburse the full amount in the form of a grant.

Most countries also provide installation allowances in the receiving area. For married workers

without children, these allowances amount to more
than a monthly wage of a lower paid worker in Sweden
and West Germany, and to less than a month's wage in
the Netherlands and the United Kingdom. Usually
there is a flat rate, and lower income groups are
not favored. Housing shortages in receiving areas
are generally a problem, but special assistance for
rehousing relocated families is effectively provided
only in Sweden.

Any consideration of financial assistance policies to promote labor mobility must give special attention to Sweden. As Eli Ginzberg has pointed out,

> There is general agreement among those
> who have studied the problem that
> Sweden has led the way in developing
> new manpower institutions, policies,
> and programs to improve the use of
> labor in a dynamic economy. Its
> Labor Market Board has an annual ap-
> propriation of about $500 million; its
> labor force is less than one-twentieth
> the size of ours. Even with an elastic
> definition of manpower programing, our
> annual federal manpower appropriation
> runs under $3 billion, making it, in
> relative terms, less than one-third
> that of Sweden's.[9]

Sweden considers its relocation assistance program to be an important part of its total employment
policy. The Labor Market Board operates the nation-
wide placement service and stimulates occupational
and geographical mobility. The 25 county labor
boards with 233 local offices provide quick information on employment changes in their respective areas.
Vacancies that cannot be filled locally are reported
to the board in Stockholm for daily publication and
distribution to all employment offices. This information is also broadcast on the radio and advertised
in the newspapers daily. Employers aid the process
by giving advance warning of layoffs. An unemployed
(or about to become unemployed) worker in a labor
surplus area, one who has no prospect of employment

in his home area, is eligible to receive a wide
variety of relocation assistance to move to an area
where manpower is needed. Workers living in the
lagging northern provinces of Sweden are entitled
to a resettlement allowance of $400 to move to more
developed parts of the country.[10]

Table 6 shows the costs of each of the various
Swedish relocation allowances for the years 1958-64.
The declining costs per person (1958-63) reflect
lower starting allowances given as the program pro-
gressed, probably because the estimated new employment duration decreased. The higher average per person cost in 1962-64 corresponds to the addition of
the resettlement allowance program. Unemployment
during this period was running at about 50,000
people (1.5 percent of the labor force); this program was thus reaching a substantial number of the
unemployed (about 30 percent).

The Swedes have found relocation assistance to
be very helpful in decreasing unemployment. Bertil
Olsson, the Labor Market Board's director general,
has remarked that

> It costs less than one million kroner
> ($200,000) to move 1,000 persons to
> employment. For the same amount,
> these persons might have been given
> employment assistance for less than
> 2 months or employed in public relief
> works for not more than 5 days. It
> can hardly be denied that the money
> is well spent when it is for removal,
> just as it cannot be denied that the
> experiment is successful.[11]

A sample of 1,091 Swedish workers receiving
starting allowances to enable them to move from
northern counties to southern counties for employment was obtained in 1963. Table 7 shows their
status one year later. Seventy-six percent were in
their initial job or another one in the same relocation area. Seven percent were in the military or had
withdrawn from the labor market. Four percent of the
sample were enrolled in job training to improve their
employment opportunities. Only 5 percent of these
formerly unemployed workers were unemployed.

TABLE 6

Relocation Allowances in Sweden, 1958-64

Year	(1) Starting Allowance		(2) Family Allowance		(3) Travel Allowance	
	Number of People	Cost ($)	Number of People	Cost ($)	Number of People	Cost ($)
1958-59	2,200	127,167	1,881	433,900	3,212	80,150
1959-60	8,164	405,000	2,110	532,000	7,465	176,300
1960-61	7,989	384,000	2,116	480,150	9,850	221,200
1961-62	8,725	441,620	2,086	428,500	12,000	303,500
1962-63	12,895	655,100	2,678	542,200	20,124	561,100
1963-64	22,290	1,837,765	3,769	878,000	38,000	1,169,750

Year	(4) Resettlement Allowance		(5) Total		(6) Average Cost Per Person ($)
	Number of People	Cost ($)	Number of People	Cost ($)	
1958-59			7,293	641,200	88
1959-60			17,739	1,113,300	63
1960-61			19,864	1,085,350	55
1961-62			22,793	1,173,600	51
1962-63	220	120,000	35,817	1,878,600	52
1963-64	1,780	642,800	55,839	4,528,300	81

Note: During this six-year period, an individual could apply for relocation assistance more than once.

Source: Martin Schnitzer, Programs for Relocating Workers Used by Governments of Selected Countries, Joint Economic Committee, 89th Congress, 2d Session, Economic Policies and Practices Paper No. 8 (Washington, D.C., 1966), pp. 29-30.

TABLE 7

Relocatees in Sweden after One Year, 1963-64

Category	Number	Percentage
Still in original job for which received starting allowance	415	38
In other employment	411	38
Unemployed	52	5
Employed in public works	17	2
In military service	44	4
Married and withdrawn from labor market or pregnant	36	3
In job-training programs	39	4
Miscellaneous	77	7
Total in sample	1,091	101*

*Total does not equal 100 percent due to rounding.

Source: Martin Schnitzer, Programs for Relocating Workers Used by Governments of Selected Countries, p. 33.

The success of the Swedish relocation program has been due to several favorable factors. The population is relatively homogeneous and high levels of employment have been prevalent. The free flow of job information between areas has been very helpful. Vocational training also has played a vital role in the total employment policy. Both labor and management support the program. Moreover there has been little political opposition from the lagging areas; this is probably because of regional development efforts in the north, which aim at broadening the area's employment potential. These efforts are concentrated on the development of three northern growth centers: Lulea, with a population of 60,000; Umeä, a university town; and Kiruna, an iron-mining

center.   In relation to relocation assistance, however, the opportunity cost is extremely high.   As
Eli Ginzberg has observed, "Even if the Swedish government could find the resources required for accelerated regional development, it is unlikely that
these small communities could be transformed into
effective growth centers.   It may not be impossible
but the costs will be high and it is difficult to
see at present how they can be met."[12]

THE UNITED STATES EXPERIENCE

Labor mobility demonstration projects conducted
under the auspices of the Department of Labor were
authorized by Congress in 1963 amendments to the
Manpower Development and Training Act of 1962.   The
purpose of these projects was to assess and demonstrate the effectiveness of a worker relocation assistance program for reducing unemployment.   Between
March 1965 and June 1969, 35 agencies, including 22
state employment services and 13 contractors, were
funded to conduct labor mobility projects in 28
states.   With the exception of three agencies that
were funded but did not relocate any workers, there
was a total of 61 projects, 40 of which were conducted by employment service agencies.   The number
of agencies and the number of projects are summarized by year in Table 8.   Projects funded in March
and April of 1965 were actually in operation and relocating workers for only three to six months.   The
"1966-67" projects were funded between April and
June of 1966 and were in operation twelve to fifteen
months.   Most projects funded in June and July of
1967 conducted relocations for at least fifteen
months.   The 1968-69 projects were all extensions
of earlier projects.[13]

The projects were designed to focus upon specific areas of high unemployment or low income as
supply areas, as well as upon areas of labor shortage as demand, or relocation, areas.   The projects
were also designed to serve specific groups of unemployed workers.   Three types of project populations were defined.   In Type A projects the population was a definable group, such as all workers

TABLE 8

Agencies Operating Labor Mobility Demonstration Projects and Number of Distinct Projects, by Type of Agency, Funding Year, and Project Population

Category	All Agencies		State Employment Services		Contractors	
	Agencies	Projects	Agencies	Projects	Agencies	Projects
Total	35[a]	61	22	40	13	21
Funding year: 1965-66	15	15	10	10	5	5
1966-67	19	21	11	13	8	8
1967-68	23	23	16	17	7	6
1968-69	6[b]	2	1	0	5	2
Project population						
General unemployed:		39		30		9
North and West	12	16	9	13	3	3
South	5	11	3	5	2	6
Appalachia	4	12	5	12	0	0
Trained workers:		11		2		9
North and West	3	6	0	0	3	6
South	2	4	1	1	1	3
Appalachia	1	1	1	1	0	0
Mass layoff:		8		7		1
Professional and technical workers	3	5	3	5	0	0
Other occupations	3	3	2	2	1	1
Urban disadvantaged	3	3	1	1	2	2

[a]The total number of agencies includes two state employment services and one contractor, which were funded but did not conduct relocations.

[b]Adequate data were available for only two contractors operating 1968-69 projects to permit inclusion in this report.

Source: Charles K. Fairchild, Worker Relocation: A Review of U.S. Department of Labor Mobility Demonstration Projects (Washington, D.C.: E. F. Shelley, 1970), p. 58.

included in a specific mass layoff or all enrollees
or graduates from a training course. Type B projects involved a predetermined portion of the labor
force, such as workers included in employment services active files. The population in Type C projects consisted of unemployed workers recruited on
the basis of their interest in relocating. In prac-
tice, distinctions among these three types tended
to disappear, particularly between Type B and Type C
populations.[14]

During the entire program there were 14,221
workers relocated, of whom 2,000 moved without relocation assistance allowances. The number of relocations and the percentage of the total relocated
by each type of agency in each funded year and in
each project population are shown in Table 9. More
than 70 percent of all workers were relocated by
state employment agencies, and about 66 percent of
these were relocated by contractor agencies. Nearly
75 percent of the workers were classified as general
unemployed, and they came from supply areas about
evenly distributed among regions. However, state
employment service projects operated primarily outside of the South, whereas contractors' projects
were found primarily in the South. Only two employment service projects focused exclusively on training graduates, while 42 percent of the workers relocated by contractors were in this category.[15]

The most comprehensive review of labor mobility
projects, that of Fairchild,[16] does not make use of
many of the tabulations that could be obtained from
records of individuals relocated by the projects.
Some of these tabulations were made by N. Dann Milne
from data made available by the Department of Labor.
Although they cover only the 1966-67 project, they
provide useful information.

In the 1966-67 projects, 10,839, or 65 percent
of the 16,644 potential relocatees contacted by
various methods, met the eligibility criteria. To
be eligible for the program a worker must have been
involuntarily unemployed, unemployed for over six
weeks regardless of cause, expecting a layoff, or a
farm worker with less than $1,200 a year family in-
come. Additionally he could not have been expected

TABLE 9

Total Relocations by Type of Agency, Funding Year, and Project Population

Category	All Agencies		State Employment Services		Contractors	
	Number	Percent	Number	Percent	Number	Percent
Total	14,221	100.0	10,196	100.0	4,025	100.0
Funding year: 1965-66	1,361	9.6	730	7.2	31	15.7
1966-67	4,129	29.0	2,627	25.8	1,502	37.3
1967-68	8,288	58.3	6,839	67.1	1,449	36.0
1968-69	443	3.1	0	0.0	443	11.0
Project population						
General unemployed:	10,236	72.0	7,923	77.7	2,313	57.6
North and West	3,294	23.2	3,127	30.7	167	4.1
South	2,975	20.9	829	8.1	2,146	53.3
Appalachia	3,967	27.9	3,967	38.9	0	0.0
Trained workers:	2,820	19.8	1,132	11.1	1,688	41.9
North and West	841	5.9	0	0.0	841	20.9
South	1,828	12.8	981	9.6	847	21.0
Appalachia	151	1.1	151	1.5	0	0.0
Mass layoff:	1,113	7.8	1,111	10.9	2	0.0
Professional and technical workers	976	6.9	976	9.6	0	0.0
Other occupations	137	1.0	135	1.3	2	0.0
Urban disadvantaged	52	0.4	30	0.3	22	0.5

Source: Charles K. Fairchild, Worker Relocation: A Review of U.S. Department of Labor Mobility Demonstration Projects (Washington, D.C.: E. F. Shelley, 1970), p. 58.

to find employment in his home area, but he could expect to obtain a job or a job offer of reasonable duration in the area of relocation. Of the persons eligible for relocation, 8,374 (77 percent) were willing to accept relocation assistance. And 1,030 expressed an interest in moving depending on the type of job or wage rate available elsewhere and/or the distance of the move. Of the eligible persons, 4,980 were referred to employers by the various agencies. Of those selected for referral, 3,981 (78 percent) accepted. In all, 3,432 workers actually accepted employment and relocated.

The project agencies were instructed to maintain contact with the relocated workers; after two months, follow-up questionnaires were administered to 2,518 relocatees. Of these, 332 (13 percent) were unemployed; 151 (6 percent) were unemployed and had returned home; and 2,069 (82 percent) expressed satisfaction with the move. This satisfaction percentage is probably overstated and should be considered to actually range between 60 and 82 percent, because of the people who were not included in the follow-up survey; they probably were not included because they no longer worked for their original employer. In any case the satisfaction or success rate seems quite good considering that all workers involved had been previously unemployed, without prospects for employment.

About half the 1966-67 mobility project relocatees were at least high school graduates, with high school graduates being the most represented of the groups shown in Table 10. The percentage of workers satisfied with their move tended to increase with rising level of education; conversely, the percentage unemployed decreased. Thus higher levels of basic education enhanced the probability of obtaining employment, probably because of greater flexibility in meeting job requirements. Of course this does not mean that selection criteria should be oriented primarily toward relocating workers who can most easily find jobs.

The data presented in Table 11 show that the projects did in fact focus on unemployed and marginal workers. Seventy-four percent of the relocatees were unemployed at the time of moving.

TABLE 10

Educational Level of Relocatees, 1966-67 Projects

Level of Education	Number Moving and Taking Job	Number of Follow-ups	Unemployed (No Prospects)		Satisfied	
			Number	Percent of Follow-ups	Number	Percent of Follow-ups
Less than 5 years	100	78	16	21	58	77
5-7 years	253	195	40	21	156	80
8 years	447	300	43	14	245	82
1-3 years high school	870	655	95	15	552	84
4 years high school	1,384	1,032	121	12	835	81
1-3 years college	265	188	15	8	161	86
4 years college	67	41	0	0	38	93

<u>Source:</u> Manpower Administration, U.S. Department of Labor.

44

TABLE 11

Employment Status of Relocatees
before Moving, 1966-67 Projects

Employment Status	Number Moving and Taking Job
Employed	
40 hours or more per week	109
20-39 hours per week	41
Less than 20 hours	37
Expecting layoff	55
Unemployed	2,456
Farm worker	140
Not in labor force	489

Source: Manpower Administration, U.S. Department of Labor.

TABLE 12

Reasons for Moving, 1966-67 Projects

Reason	Number of Relocatees	Percent	Percent Satisfied with Move
No local employment	2,259	90	83
Family reasons	54	2	86
Community reasons	62	2	88
Employment and family reasons	62	2	74
Employment and community reasons	27	1	86
Family and community reasons	46	2	74

Source: Manpower Administration, U.S. Department of Labor.

Those employed were eligible because they were farm
workers or persons making less than $1,200 a year.
The data in Table 12 show that, among reasons for
moving, "no local employment" accounted for 90 percent of the responses and was a contributing factor
in another 3 percent. The locational preferences
of the relocatees were also analyzed, but they are
considered separately (see Chapter 3).

A vital concomitant to simple relocation assistance is manpower training. It is not sufficient
merely to help an unemployed worker move to an area
where jobs are available, because low education and
skill levels tend to decrease the possibility of
obtaining satisfactory employment for the relocatee.
Thus much of the effectiveness of a relocation program depends upon upgrading the skills and education levels of the relocatees. In the 1966-67 projects an average of 47 percent of the applicants accepting job referral were Manpower Development and
Training Act (MDTA) trainees. An average of 53 percent of these were placed in the same vocation as
their training (see Table 13). This was below the
1966 national average of approximately 60 percent,
and it points up an area for improvement in future
relocation programs.

The data in Table 14 indicate that the most
frequently encountered problem in the various relocation projects was difficulty in finding suitable
housing at a reasonable price for the relocatee.
Aid in securing housing, therefore, should be a
major part of the comprehensive assistance provided
by a continuous program of relocation. In the 1966-
67 projects only 32 percent of the relocatees received assistance in finding housing. Many rural-
to-urban relocatees did not even know that either
rental agencies with multiple listings or public
housing were available. Liaison with appropriate
rental agencies and public housing authorities (or
with boarding houses for single people) could be
easily and inexpensively maintained by the employment service.

Table 15 shows the starting wages of those relocated in the various projects. There is a direct
relationship between percentage of relocatees who

TABLE 13

MDTA Training and Job Placement of Applicants
Accepting Job Referral, 1966-67 Projects

Occupation	Number	Those Placed in Same Vocation	
		Number	Percent
Professionals, technicians, and managers	159	73	46
Managers and proprietors	96	44	46
Clerical	154	76	49
Service	111	49	44
Agricultural	31	15	48
Processing	16	2	13
Benchwork	80	25	31
Machine trades	533	329	62
Structural	461	266	58
Miscellaneous	62	18	29
Total	1,703	897	53

Source: Manpower Administration, U.S. Department of Labor.

TABLE 14

Relocatees Expressing Significant Problems
with Moving, 1966-67 Projects

Problem	Number	Percent*
Relocation expenses	122	5
Financial problems	287	11
Job adjustment	179	7
Housing problems	429	17
Personal and/or family problems	187	7
Other	83	3

*The percent is based on 2,518 follow-up interviews.

Source: Manpower Administration, U.S. Department of Labor.

remained in their jobs and the wage level. Among
the alternatives to their new employment, the relocatees had the possibility of employment in their
home area, another job in the new location, unemployment compensation, and Work Experience and Training Program payments. In many cases, rural-to-urban
migrants found the cost of food, utilities, and housing (especially if they had owned their home in the
supply area) higher. It is not surprising then that
many of the lower-wage earners decided that their
new real income was not sufficient to overcome the
economic and noneconomic costs of being away from
home.

    Finally the importance of relocation assistance
as an inducement to move is illustrated by the data
presented in Table 16. Fifty-two percent of the
follow-up questionnaire respondents indicated that
they would not have moved without the relocation allowance; only 14 percent indicated that the allowance did not in any way alter their decision to move.

    On the basis of his analysis of the 1966-67
projects, Milne concludes that

> society benefits greatly from these
> relocation projects. Of course, re-
> location programs should not totally
> replace subsidies to bring employment
> to rural areas or welfare payments.
> These pilot projects show that there
> is a sizable group of unemployed
> workers who are willing to relocate
> to obtain employment. Providing re-
> location assistance to these people is
> the least expensive governmental method
> of providing employment for them. For
> those unwilling or unable to move, un-
> employment insurance and welfare pay-
> ments will be available. What is im-
> portant is giving the unemployed
> worker a choice, rather than condemn-
> ing him to unemployment because he
> lacks the means to relocate to areas
> where employment is available.[17]

TABLE 15

Starting Hourly Wages of Relocatees,
1966-67 Projects

Hourly Wage	Number	Percentage Still in Job at Follow-up Survey
Under $1.50	591	50
$1.50-$1.99	685	51
$2.00-$2.49	1,043	63
$2.50-$2.99	559	72
$3.00-$3.49	307	87
$3.50-$3.99	127	88
$4.00-$4.49	38	84
$4.50 and over	68	93

Source: Manpower Administration, U.S. Department of Labor.

TABLE 16

Importance of Relocation Allowances to
Relocatees, 1966-67 Projects

Category	Number	Percent
Would not have moved without it	1,176	52
Made relocation decision earlier, but might have moved without it	348	15
Would have moved anyway, but allowance permitted earlier move	427	19
Would have moved anyway, no difference in timing of move	313	14
Total	2,264	100

Source: Manpower Administration, U.S. Department of Labor.

In Charles Fairchild's review of the Department of Labor mobility demonstration projects, it is estimated that total expenditures on the entire program were about $13 million. Of this total, $12.3 million was spent directly by individual projects, $4.2 million went for relocation assistance allowances, and $8.1 million was spent for project administration. These figures represent an average expenditure of $867 per relocated worker, of which $294 was for relocation assistance allowances and $573 for administrative expenses.[18]

Fairchild's conclusions, which are in accord with the author's personal investigations of several projects, merit detailed discussion because of their potential relevance to future relocation assistance programs in the United States. It will be recalled that the only persons eligible for relocation assistance allowances in the mobility projects were involuntarily unemployed workers without local prospects for jobs, members of farm families with an income of less than $1,200 a year, and persons having only occasional odd job employment. It is recommended that a permanent program extend eligibility criteria to include underemployed persons working less than full time or working full time at low wages, and to fully employed persons earning incomes below the poverty level.[19]

Although the mobility projects required a definite job offer in the receiving area before relocation assistance allowances were paid, they did not require certification of a shortage of workers in the relevant occupations in these areas. It is recommended that in a permanent program, allowances be granted to individuals only for relocation to jobs in occupations in which there is a certified shortage of workers in the receiving area. It is also recommended that consideration be given to limiting assistance to the amount required for a move to the nearest labor market in which an eligible individual could be placed in a suitable job. This limitation would tend to discourage unnecessarily long moves and would reduce allowance costs. Individuals who do not meet the recommended eligibility criteria but who still wish to move using their own

resources should be provided with information about
employment opportunities in other labor markets and
also should be provided with other nonfinancial assistance in order to make their moves as efficient
as possible.

The importance of nonfinancial supportive assistance to relocatees appears to be at least as important as financial assistance. Job information and
placement services play a crucial role in relocating
workers and directing moves in economically rational
directions. Preemployment interview trips were an
effective tool in obtaining information about available jobs in various areas. Grants for such trips
should be made to workers on a per diem basis for
interviews with potential employers identified
through the job development process. Other supportive services that many disadvantaged workers need
include personal and family counseling, budgeting
advice, and especially assistance in locating housing.

The need for a comprehensive approach in relating relocatees to their communities cannot be over-
emphasized. As Fairchild puts it,

> Perhaps the most important lesson
> learned by agencies conducting relo-
> cation projects, Employment Services
> and contractors alike, was that suc-
> cessfully placing workers in jobs in
> other areas requires more than simply
> matching workers with jobs. It also
> requires matching the worker and his
> spouse, if any, with the demand area
> community. Projects learned through
> bad experiences the importance of
> ascertaining the attitude of the
> spouse toward relocation in general
> and toward moving to specific area.[20]

The experience of the pilot mobility projects
has demonstrated that in a permanent relocation assistance program, one agency should have responsibility for worker relocation. The federal-state
employment service is the obvious choice, because
it has offices across the nation, has expertise in

job development and placement, and is the major pro-
vider of manpower services in the nation. The only
alternative would be to create a new agency that
would duplicate many of the functions of the employment service.

Moreover the existing systems for collecting
and distributing information about job openings are
inadequate. Important advances are being made in
computer information banks, but these banks will
not cover smaller metropolitan areas or rural areas
for some time. An interim solution to the problem
of linking supply and demand areas might be to place
greater reliance on direct telephone inquiries for
the purpose of acquiring information about jobs and
workers. Increased use also should be made of pre-
employment travel grants that permit job seekers to
have face-to-face interviews with prospective employers and to examine the community in which available jobs are located.[21]

It is not recommended that there be tests that
relate eligibility for assistance to the financial
means of a worker to move without assistance or to
his projected earnings after relocation. Such tests
violate the concept that a relocation program should
operate to improve the utilization of manpower resources. In particular, groups whose earnings may
be relatively high after relocation may be making
the greatest contribution to total production from
a national point of view. Similarly it is not recommended that relocated workers be required to repay
allowances, although penalties, of course, should be
assessed in case of fraud. The mobility projects
did, in fact, require repayment of allowances by
workers who did not remain on their jobs or in the
areas in which they were placed. This method has
been used in Sweden to prevent workers from relocating repeatedly. However, given existing imper-
fections in information and methods, it is not always clear in cases where relocated individuals returned home whether the fault was with them or with
the program. Nevertheless it is important to emphasize again that if worker relocation is to increase
opportunities for persons with limited prospects for
employment in the local labor market, it should be

integrated into a comprehensive program of vocational and nonvocational services.[22]

In view of Fairchild's generally favorable view
of the results of the labor mobility projects, it is
appropriate to cite the conclusions of a similar, if
not quite so comprehensive, evaluation by Garth
Mangum:

> [A mobility assistance] program would
> provide no major solution to unemploy-
> ment but it would be important for
> those who choose to take advantage of
> it. The disadvantaged as well as the
> advantaged should have a meaningful
> geographical dimension to their free-
> dom of occupational choice. Their
> geographic mobility is currently high
> but often irrational. A major contri-
> bution of a publicly supported program
> should be reduction of randomness.
> The preliminary MDTA experience indi-
> cates that relocation assistance,
> financial and nonfinancial, is a use-
> ful and needed tool in the total kit
> of manpower policy measures.[23]

Because of the importance attached to
intermediate-sized cities in this book, it is important to emphasize that most of the demonstration
projects were designed to help persons move from
nonmetropolitan areas to either nearby metropolitan areas or regional growth centers. This effort
apparently was successful. Already in 1968, Audrey
Freedman's analysis of the projects concluded that

> By providing an unemployed person with
> specific job offers, and some moving
> money, the projects have prevented the
> arrival of an unemployed worker, with
> little or no funds, at a city where it
> may take him weeks or months to find a
> job. The services necessary to create
> a planned move for him will differ ac-
> cording to his education, experience,

family size and age, and cultural background. Some of the larger projects
are beginning to divert unwise, goal-
less moves in the direction of medium-
sized cities where labor demand is
strong and the chances for adjustment
are better.[24]

By the time of Fairchild's more recent analysis,
more than 80 percent of the relocated workers had
come from nonmetropolitan areas and most of these
went to metropolitan areas within the same state.
At the time of the standard two-month follow-up
period, 75 percent of the relocated workers had remained in the areas to which they had moved, though
they were not always in their original jobs. Fairchild points out that "projects designed to redirect
the geographic mobility out of rural areas toward
nearby employment opportunities and away from traditional urban destinations were able to do so,"[25]
and that "These efforts appear to have been most
successful in projects relocating workers from rural
to small metropolitan areas."[26] In the light of
this experience it is recommended that "a permanent
program should concentrate the bulk of its resources
in relocating workers to nearby growth centers."[27]

IMPLEMENTING AND DELIVERING
WORKER RELOCATION SERVICES[28]

The basic objective of worker relocation assistance is to match an unemployed worker who is not
able to find a job locally with a job for which he
can qualify, and to move the worker to the job. Of
course, the relocation process involves much more
than simply moving people to new locations. During
initial screening and prior to moving the potential
relocatees need a wide variety of prerelocation supportive services, such as personal and family counseling, testing, and medical and dental examinations.
On the other hand, a wide variety of services must
be developed in the demand area. Post-relocation
supportive services include legal advice, financial

counseling, personal counseling, general orientation
to the new area, medical and dental services, transportation, and information about schools and day-
care facilities, additional training, and welfare
services.

Past experience with labor mobility demonstration projects has shown that in most cases supportive services will succeed or fail according to the
degree to which effective communications can be established between demand and supply area staffs.
It has been emphasized time and time again that Wide
Area Telephone Service is necessary to communicate
employer needs and/or relocatee availability immediately. It is also critical that relocatee needs be
met quickly. In general, the importance of mini-
mizing time lags during the relocation process cannot be minimized.

Training programs for relocation project staff
members should fully acquaint their staff members
with the characteristics of disadvantaged people.
It is particularly important to understand the attitudes of these people concerning their self image,
group feelings and observations, authority, achieve-
ment, religion, prestige rules, and innovations.
This demands not only human relations skills but
also skills in the techniques of interviewing. Frequently, those who work with disadvantaged persons
make the erroneous assumption that a "job" creates
the motivation necessary to succeed, and that any-
one lacking this motivation must be lazy or shift-
less. This attitude of course reflects middle-class
cultural views, and most programs are in fact designed by people with middle- or upper-class back-
grounds. In their environment money can be counted
on as an important motivating force, but this is
not necessarily the case with poor people. Too
often they have become unaccustomed to planning for
tomorrow because their energies have been devoted
to scraping together the bare essentials of life.
This problem will vary from person to person, but
worker relocation staff members must be prepared to
deal with its many manifestations.

Regardless of the staffing and service models
appropriate to a particular project, certain functions

must be performed in both the supply and demand areas if the relocation effort is to be successful. Supply area functions and activities include the following:

1. identifying and recruiting potential relocatees who are involuntarily unemployed or underemployed,

2. ascertaining the availability of local suitable employment for the potential relocatee,

3. ascertaining whether or not suitable employment opportunities exist in the demand area or areas,

4. providing pre-relocation counseling to each applicant (and his family, if married) concerning relocation for employment, services offered by the project, potential problems in the demand area and in the moving process, and the overall purpose and intent of relocation,

5. coordinating with potential relocatees the means by which they can pay off old debts,

6. arranging for pre-employment interviews in the demand area,

7. initiating requests for appropriate financial assistance,

8. coordinating and assisting relocatees in packing, loading, and moving household goods,

9. coordinating and assisting transportation from the supply area, and

10. investigating the reasons why some relocatees have returned home.

On the demand side, staff functions and activities would include:

1. conducting outreach job development to obtain suitable employment opportunities for target population applicants, and thoroughly explaining all program activities to each prospective employer,

2. ascertaining availability of local workers to fill jobs in the demand area,

3. notifying the supply area staff of available jobs,

4. helping workers with pre-employment interviews,

5. processing financial assistance when workers accept employment,

      6. arranging for public transportation to and from the job site or assisting with the purchase or repair of an automobile,

      7. dispersing financial assistance,

      8. assisting in finding suitable housing,

      9. assisting in the purchasing of basic household goods if needed,

      10. helping the applicant and his family move into their new home,

      11. performing counseling services and assisting in a wide variety of adjustment problems in the demand area, and

      12. conducting follow-up activities as needed. Moreover, it is essential that daily telephone contact be maintained between demand and supply areas.

      In the past it has been found that staff members engaged in worker relocation activities should have certain characteristics particularly needed in this kind of activity. The supply area coordinator should be knowledgeable about and able to accept the cultural traits of the target population. It is also helpful if his socioeconomic background is similar to or identical with that of the target population. He should be able to develop and maintain an accurate and up-to-date inventory of supportive services in the supply area and he should be capable of working without supervision and close support. He should be willing to live with a fluctuating work schedule depending on the needs of potential relocatees. The demand area coordinator should be able to communicate effectively with potential employers, and therefore should have a relatively high level of education. He should be able to supervise staff activities effectively and he should have an understanding of the problems of disadvantaged people. The overall project supervisor should possess all of these characteristics and have more education and experience than his staff. Otherwise, he may not be able to supervise staff activities effectively.

      Any serious worker relocation effort needs considerable prior planning. Target populations must be identified and defined, and careful attention must be paid to the kinds of problems they are

encountering at present, as well as those they are
likely to encounter if they undertake relocation.
The program of supportive services must be geared
to these actual and potential problems. Among the
more important factors that need to be considered
are age, education, past failure or success in relocation efforts, and ethnic factors. If the individual derives his identity from his ethnic group
any attempt simply to divorce him from this group
will and probably should fail. It is important to
know what supportive services may be available in
both supply and demand areas. Constructive dialogue
should also be opened with leadership groups in both
areas. In the supply area it should be recognized
that no leader--political or otherwise--enjoys losing constituents, and that communications failures
may result in services not being utilized by those
who most need them. On the other hand, failure to
work with the leadership in receiving areas may well
result in the rejection of relocatees by the community.

In general, successful relocation efforts require the effective performance of five activities:
recruitment, screening, job development, transitional services, follow-up, and supportive services.

Recruitment efforts should solicit the support
of community leaders and all manpower and related
agencies. In many cases it is useful to bring in
employers from demand areas for radio and television
appearances and press interviews. In areas where
manpower programs are less developed more intensive
recruitment efforts may be necessary. In these circumstances, door to door contacts, referrals through
friends, community organizations and other agencies,
and broad mass media appeals may be used.

The screening process must determine whether an
individual would benefit from or is interested in
relocation assistance services. Indeed, most failures in relocation can be traced to malfunctioning
in this process. During the screening process attention must be paid to age, size of family, indebt-
edness, welfare dependency, degree of literacy,
health, amount of property owned, degree of social
and physical isolation, and previous employment

experience. Both the degree of financial assistance
and the supportive services offered to a worker and
his family depend on his situation with respect to
these variables. It should be remembered that many
disadvantaged people have been visited by persons
who were going to "help" them, yet they have remained poor. As a result, there often is considerable apprehension concerning programs which are supposed to help them move out of poverty. During the
screening process, the opinions of friends, community
leaders, and former employers should be used to sup-
plement those of the supply area staff. In addition,
tests that might aid in identifying problems requir-
ing professional assistance might prove useful. The
results of these tests should be forwarded to the
demand area so that the staff there can provide the
necessary supportive services. In general, it should
be remembered that the screening process should be
designed not so much to screen out individuals as to
screen in persons who can be helped by relocation
assistance and a comprehensive program of supportive
services.

In the job development process, it is important
to make the relocation alternative real to the potential relocatee. Current information on job openings is essential so that the potential relocatee
can be presented with a definite job and an identi-
fiable employer, rather than just a possible job
with one or another employer. (A valuable contribution would be made in this regard by a computerized
job bank.) Another aspect of the job development
process is relating job openings to the individual's
whole profile of needs and problems. This should
involve working with employers who are not only interested in relaxing entry requirements, but also
in developing an ability to understand and take account of the special needs and problems of relocatees.
Moreover, if the relocatee is to acquire a long-
range view he should be given a job that has a definite prospect for upward mobility.

Transitional services are all those made necessary by the physical relocation of the worker and
his family. Delivery of these services begins when
relocation becomes a serious alternative for the

individual. Transitional services delivered in the
supply area include pre-relocation counseling, orien·
tation to the area of relocation, and the processing
and payment of any pre-employment interview expense
allowances to which the worker may be entitled.
Other pre-relocation transitional services may include disposing of old debts, help in terminating
leases or disposing of property, and assistance in
making arrangements for the move, such as contacting
the moving company or making arrangements to get the
family car in shape for the trip. Difficulty in
overcoming these seemingly small problems is often
the reason why the family has not moved earlier.
The transitional services that are to be provided
promptly in the demand area include payment of relocation assistance allowances, assistance in finding suitable housing, help in making preliminary
contacts in the community, aid in getting the worker
to his job the first few days, assistance in enroll-
ing the children in school, and help with the family
shopping. Here, too, careful attention must be paid
to the resolution of apparently elementary problems.
     The purpose of follow-up and supportive ser-
vices is to promote successful adjustment of the
worker to his job, and of the worker and his family
to the community. Follow-up on an as-needed basis
is often appropriate for up to six months and sometimes even longer. Follow-up contact with the
worker, his employer, and his family will often result in the identification of problems of the transitional type that were not encountered during the immediate post-relocation period. In a new community,
it is difficult for the relocatee to slice through
the maze of agencies, organizations, and regulations
pertaining to services he may need. This is especially true if the relocatee is disadvantaged. Assistance from the demand area staff is frequently
required to prevent the relocatee from becoming dis-
couraged and returning to the more familiar ways of
home.
     For most jobs of any consequence or offering
any upward mobility, little hiring is done without
a pre-employment interview. Most employers insist
on seeing a man before hiring him, and few workers

want to take a job sight unseen. Moreover, a worker
is more likely to take a job and stick with his decision if his wife has participated in the pre-
employment interview trip as well as in the decision to relocate. During the pre-employment interview trip, the worker and his wife should have the
opportunity to look over available housing and to
gain some acquaintance of the community at large.
Details concerning lodging and transportation during the pre-employment interview trip should be
handled by the demand area staff so that the relocatee and his wife are not distracted by logistical
details.

Once a worker has accepted a job offer and a
reporting date is agreed upon, the expenses associated with relocation to the job site become identi-
fiable. There are four different categories of relocation expense allowances. First are the travel
and per diem costs of the worker and his family
while in transit or awaiting the availability of
suitable housing or the arrival of household goods.
Second are the costs of transporting the worker's
possessions. Third are out-of-pocket expenses for
such items as rent and utility deposits, required
supplies, groceries, and basic appliances. Fourth
are optional costs such as those involved in acquiring a house or a mobile home; acquiring an automobile, or putting a currently owned automobile in
dependable running order; and the payment of old
debts. Regardless of the system used to compute
allowances in any or all of these four categories,
it is important that they be paid promptly and at
the time that the expenses are incurred. Few relocatees have ready means to cover these expenses;
otherwise, they probably would have moved on their
own. Insofar as possible it would be desirable to
have service vendors bill the demand area staff
agency directly. This relieves the relocatee of
having to contend with this problem during the
critical relocation period, and it simplifies audit
and control procedures.

To be eligible for relocation assistance allowances, a worker should be involuntarily unemployed
or underemployed and unable to obtain work locally,

be at least 18 years old, and, of course, be willing
to relocate. Before the payment of any allowances
other than pre-employment interview expense allowances, it should be ascertained that the worker has
obtained a job in the demand area community. It
should also be established that his wage will meet
or exceed the federal minimum wage or the wage prevailing in the community for similar work. It
should also be ascertained that the new job will
provide sufficient resources to maintain a reasonable standard of living in the area of relocation.

The objective of relocation cannot be achieved
unless the relocatee is guaranteed a satisfactory
year around income. The job that he receives should
have good long-range potential. Relocation of workers to jobs in declining industries or to dying occupations in growing industries may solve some
short-run problems, but may lead to greater difficulty in the long run. If there are workers residing in the demand area who have the same qualifica-
tions as the relocatee, then they should have first
preference for any relevant job opening. To relocate people to such jobs would not be consistent
with an overall manpower program; moreover, the
fact that these jobs remain open despite the availability of suitable workers might indicate that
they are, in fact, dead-end jobs. Finally, to the
extent possible, employers should be sought out who
offer attractive fringe benefit packages and who
demonstrate genuine social concern. This obviously
will ease the task of the demand area staff in working out problems besetting the relocated worker and
his family.

SUMMARY AND CONCLUSIONS

The United States, like nearly all other in-
dustrialized nations of the West, has a fairly well-
developed system of aids to promote the growth of
economically lagging regions. Unlike most comparable nations, however, it does not have a permanent
program to help underemployed, unemployed, and low
income persons in lagging areas to move and find

employment in areas with greater opportunities. European experience with relocation assistance, particularly in Sweden, together with labor mobility demonstration projects in the United States, have shown that such programs are effective in helping the target populations and in improving overall national manpower utilization. Failure to institute a permanent program of comprehensive relocation assistance is perhaps the most deficient aspect of the complex of policies designed to promote more rational spatial resource allocation in the United States.

At the beginning of this book it was argued that it is inefficient and ineffective to try to promote the industrialization of many lagging rural areas and small towns. It is often equally wasteful in both human and economic terms for persons from these areas to migrate to large metropolitan areas. However, migration to growing intermediate cities (intermediate with respect to both size and location) does represent a viable alternative for many of these persons. Several of the labor mobility demonstration projects have clearly indicated the feasibility of rechanneling migration streams away from the traditional paths that too frequently lead the movers to big cities with no definite job prospects, toward intermediate growth centers, usually located in the same state as the movers' home communities. These limited projects did not, of course, indicate the degree to which residents of lagging rural areas and small towns actually prefer to go to intermediate centers, in contrast to the alternatives of staying home or going to the big city, although some information was obtained on the locational preferences of persons relocated through the projects (see Chapter 3). There thus remain the questions of the degree to which persons still living in lagging areas prefer to move, the extent to which they actually expect to move, and their preferred destinations if they prefer or expect to move. These issues are dealt with in detail in the next two chapters.

3

LOCATION PREFERENCE STUDIES—
THEIR NATURE,
SIGNIFICANCE,
AND LIMITATIONS

INTRODUCTION

According to the most familiar definition of the discipline, economics is the study of the allocation of scarce resources among competing uses. An equally familiar tenet is that economics provides the tools to guide individuals or even societies in selecting the composition and timing of consumption and investment that maximizes total satisfaction insofar as this is possible through essentially material, if not necessarily hedonistic, means. Within these and related contexts one finds no lack of discussion concerning the who, what, how, and when of production and consumption (or investment and saving). But the <u>where</u> factor is usually conspicuously absent, as though the spatial dimension of human existence were somehow homogeneous or irrelevant.

There has been a virtual explosion of output in the regional and urban economics fields during the past decade, before which time there was available solely the work of a relatively few pioneers. Whereas only a few universities offered courses in these fields a decade ago, such courses are now an almost universally accepted part of the offerings of most graduate programs of university study. (Because they both deal with problems of the geographic dimensions of economic activity, regional and urban economics probably should be melded into a common area of study; it could be termed, _faute de mieux_, spatial economics, though a better appellation must surely be available in an age when "spatial" is generally associated with space vehicles.)   Still, in contrast to the attention that has been given to time preferences of consumers and locational preferences of firms, for example, it is remarkable that so little attention has been given to the residential location preferences of individuals or to how the geographic organization of economic activities may be brought more into line with the preferences of people.

This chapter reviews some residential locational preference studies that have been made in France and the United States, and critically examines the methodology employed in our studies of the location preferences of Appalachian, Indian, Mexican American, and Mississippi (black and white) high school seniors.   The results of our studies are discussed in detail in the next chapter.

RESIDENTIAL PREFERENCES IN FRANCE

The high degree of concentration of French population and economic activity in the Paris region has been discussed at length by the author elsewhere.[1] During the past decade the French government has initiated a series of policies designed to check the growth of population and industry in the Paris region—which nearly all Frenchmen regard as overcrowded[2]—and to bring increased vitality to lagging provincial regions, particularly in the southwest.   For planning purposes France has been divided into 21 program regions, and the national budget is regionalized annually in terms of these regions.   A strategic plan has been prepared to guide the development of the Paris region, but measures have been taken to stimulate growth in provincial areas.   One approach is to build up the tertiary activities of cities in the Paris basin (Rouen, Le Havre, Caen, Le Mans, Tours, Orléans, Troyes, Reims, and Amiens) and to support their industrial growth in order to sharply reduce migration

from the basin to Paris and to make the basin a
zone of attraction for migrants from the rest of
France. An even more ambitious effort to provide
a balance to the pull of the Paris region is represented by the eight métropoles d'équilibres that
have been chosen for special development aid. They
are Lyon-St. Etienne; Marseille-Aix; Bordeaux;
Lille-Roubaix-Tourcoing; Toulouse; Strasbourg;
Nantes-St. Nazaire; and Nancy-Metz.

The coordination of regional planning efforts
at the national level is the responsibility of the
Delegation for Spatial Planning and Regional Action
(Délégation à l'aménagement du territoire et à
l'action régionale, or DATAR). This interministe-
rial agency is not an administrative body in the
usual sense; rather, in its tasks of coordination
and impulsion, it works closely with the nation's
General Planning Commission.[3]

The French have not only the most comprehensive
national system of regional planning in the Atlantic
Community, but also have given considerable attention to the locational preferences of people
throughout the nation. Moreover these preferences
are taken into account relatively frequently in
French discussions of regional planning efforts.

Since its creation in 1945 the National Institute for Demographic Studies in Paris has made several surveys to study the level of information and
attitudes of the French public concerning demographic
problems. In 1965 a well-designed survey was made of
2,541 persons in 198 localities. Proportional sampling was employed with respect to age, sex, community
size, region, and occupation of family head. Among
other questions, the respondents were asked the following: "In your opinion, are questions concerning
the population of France, that is to say the number
and distribution of people and the changes that could
take place, very important, important, of little importance, or of no importance?" The results are given
in Table 17 according to the level of information
of the respondents. The level of information was
determined by asking five very general questions
about the size, composition, and growth of France's

TABLE 17

Importance Attached by Frenchmen to
Questions of Population, 1965
(percentage)

| Degree of Importance | Level of Information | | | |
	Well Informed	Little Informed	Badly Informed	All Levels
Very important	39	32	17	30
Important	46	41	36	41
Little importance	2	6	9	6
No importance	5	4	8	5
No response	8	17	30	18
Total	100	100	100	100

Source: Henri Bastide and Alain Girard, "Les tendances démographiques en France et les attitudes de la population," Population, XXI, 1 (January-February 1966), 19.

population; well-informed respondents answered at least four questions correctly, whereas badly-informed respondents were not able to answer more than one question correctly. As may be expected, level of information was closely related to amount of education. Seventy-one percent of the persons interviewed believed that population questions are important or very important; these responses were given by 85 percent of the well-informed persons, in contrast to only 53 percent of those badly-informed.

In the same survey, respondents were asked if they generally had sufficient means to satisfy their personal and family needs. Sixty-four percent stated that their means were either "insufficient" or "very insufficient." Persons in these groups were then asked if they would be willing to move to a different region if they could thereby obtain sufficient means. About 50 percent of these persons were willing to move. This proportion was found in both rural areas and provincial cities

regardless of size. In Paris, however, more than
50 percent of the dissatisfied would move--a proportion amounting to 35 percent of the agglomera-
tion's population. This may be due in large measure to the fact that Paris contains a relatively
high proportion of immigrants, and past studies
have indicated that persons who have already migrated are more likely to migrate again than are
potential first-time migrants.[4]

Given the high degree of potential mobility in
France, the question of where people would prefer
to live becomes significant. In the 1965 survey
the respondents were asked: "If you had the choice,
and if you could have the same means as you now
have ('à condition de disposer des mêmes ressources')
would you prefer to live in the Paris region, a
large provincial city, a small provincial city, or
a rural area?" The responses, by actual place of
residence class, are presented in Table 18. They
indicate that most people would prefer to remain
where they are or in a locality of more or less
similar size. The principal exception is the Paris
region, where only 42 percent would choose to remain where they are. (Of the persons living in
cities with more than 100,000 inhabitants, only 40
percent would choose a large provincial city; but
this does not necessarily mean they are dissatisfied
with their current place of residence, because many
may regard their city as a "small city" rather than
a "large provincial city." Seventy percent of the
respondents in cities with more than 100,000 persons would choose one or the other of these alternatives.) It is relevant to note that of all the
subgroups sampled other than the Paris group, the
proportion that would choose to live in the Paris
region ranges from a minimum of 3 percent to a maximum of only 8 percent. The proportion of the entire national sample preferring to live in Paris is
only 11 percent.

A similar survey made in 1959-60 also showed
that the persons who would most willingly leave
their present location were the Parisians. The results likewise showed that the people of other regions of heavy urban concentration, such as Flanders,

TABLE 18

Preferred Place of Residence by Actual
Place of Residence, France, 1965
(percentage)

Preferred Residence	Rural	2,000 to 20,000	20,000 to 100,000	Over 100,000	Paris Region	Total
Rural	68	31	25	22	23	42
Small city	22	42	52	30	16	29
Large provincial city	7	18	16	40	15	17
Paris	3	8	6	6	42	11
No response	0	1	1	2	4	1
Total	100	100	100	100	100	100

Source: Bastide and Girard, op. cit., p. 32.

Artois, and the Lyon region, had relatively high
preferences to live elsewhere. On the basis of
this survey it was concluded that

> If the expressed aspirations could be
> satisfied, the movement away from the
> countryside, however vigorously con-
> demned, would continue, but a regroup-
> ment would be made to the profit of
> medium and large provincial cities,
> and Paris would cease to grow. Thus,
> one of the most important results of
> this study is that decentralization
> efforts conform to the wishes of the
> population.[5]

A comparably designed survey made in 1963 indicated
that, given actual growth trends, public opinion

favored government action to curb the growth of the
Paris region. This attitude was expressed by two-
thirds of the respondents living in provincial regions and by a slightly higher proportion of those
living in the Paris region.[6]

As the author has pointed out in a previous
study,[7] whether or not these phenomena should be of
concern to economists depends on the nature of the
problems and issues behind these responses. The
1963 survey posed this question to Paris respondents: "In your opinion, what are the three most
harmful or disagreeable things that one experiences
in Paris and the surrounding urban area?" Over
one-third of the responses mentioned atmospheric
pollution or similar health hazards (43 percent),
traffic problems (41 percent), noise (34 percent),
and unsatisfactory public transportation (34 percent). Such other problems as cost of living and
tempo of life were mentioned in only 20 percent or
fewer of the replies. Thus, despite the fact that
many social scientists have given considerable attention to the analysis of such allegedly "urban"
phenomena as hyperintensity of individual and social behavior, absence of satisfactory social relations, egocentrism, and the like, these factors
were not cited frequently in the Paris responses.
It may be that problems of a sociological or psychological nature were more important than the
people themselves realized. However, if government
policy is to respond to expressed preferences,
these findings imply that policy should be oriented
toward the amelioration of problems that are largely
economic in nature, for the common element in the
major grievances of Paris residents is space economy.

It is not surprising, therefore, that Bastide
and Girard conclude that "if aspirations, as they
have been expressed, could be realized, the present
population distribution would be significantly modified."[8] They point out that:

> Rural areas and small towns with a
> semi-rural character would definitely
> keep their same importance, but in
> any case the migratory movement

toward the cities would not be reversed. The large provincial cities
would likewise maintain their present
relative status. But the Paris region would lose its attraction at the
expense of small cities.

In the final analysis the movement toward concentration in Paris
does not seem to correspond to deep
aspirations, even though people still
are moving there. But it is important
to note that the attraction of the
large provincial cities should not be
minimized in the perspective of the
development of important regional
metropolitan centers.[9]

This evaluation was based on a comparison of
preferred residences with actual population distribution at the time of the 1962 census. Between
1962 and 1968 the population of the Paris region
grew by 750,000 (that of the city proper declined
by 200,000), but this was only two-thirds of the
increase that had been officially predicted.[10] According to a recent document outlining the regional
planning orientations for the new sixth plan (1971-
75), the significant slowing in the growth of the
Paris region has been accompanied by marked growth
in most parts of the Paris basin. The arrival of
an unanticipated number of repatriated persons from
North Africa during the 1960s reinforced the growth
of the regions along the Mediterranean. Meanwhile
the lagging regions of western France had twice the
rate of population growth between 1962 and 1968
that they experienced between 1954 and 1962, and
for the first time in generations they appeared to
have a positive net migration rate. Throughout
France there has been a recent vigorous growth of
cities in the 30,000-200,000 range, fed by surplus
rural population and accompanied by strong growth
in the manufacturing and tertiary sectors. To what
extent these phenomena have been a consequence of
regional policy efforts and to what extent they
have been "spontaneous" is a matter of conjecture.

Nevertheless the planners believe such phenomena
are in no small measure the fruits of policies that
have been formulated with public preferences in
mind. They are now at work considering the direct
and indirect effects on population distribution of
population growth, urban expansion, economic inno-
vation, technological change, the opening of fron-
tiers to increased trade, and the development of
leisure activities. And there is still general
agreement that "there is a real danger that spontaneous localizations can lead to undesirable concentrations that result in urban congestion, satu-
rated public facilities, aggravated nuisances, and
degradation of modes of living if they are not cor-
rected by a more vigorous planning policy."[11]

RESIDENTIAL PREFERENCES IN
THE UNITED STATES

A Gallup Poll survey made in February 1970
asked the following question: "If you could live
anywhere in the United States that you wanted to,
would you prefer a city, suburban area, small town,
or farm?" The results, by selected groups, are
shown in Table 19. Whereas 55 percent of the respondents preferred to live in a small town or on a
farm, only 44 percent preferred a city or suburban
residence. A similar Gallup Poll survey in 1966
indicated that these relative preferences were about
evenly split; 50 percent favored the city or suburb
and 49 percent favored the small town or farm.
Thus during this four-year interval there was a
definite trend in preferences toward the small town
or farm in contrast to the actual trend toward
greater urbanization.

In the 1970 survey the city found relative favor among nonwhites, residents of the East, and
persons already residing in communities with a population greater than 50,000. The farm was favored
by 56 percent of the rural respondents and by 85
percent of the farmers. Thus while there was a
tendency for people to prefer, at least relatively,
the kind of place in which they already lived, more

TABLE 19

Gallup Poll Results of Residential Preferences of Americans, by Selected Groups, February 1970

(percentage)

Residential Preference	All Groups	Sex		Race		Education			Occupation				Age		
		Men	Women	White	Nonwhite	College	High School	Grade School	Prof. & Bus.	White Collar	Farmers	Manual	21-29 years	30-49 years	50 & over
City	18	17	20	17	28	22	17	17	21	22	0	17	19	16	20
Suburban area	26	25	26	25	31	30	27	20	30	33	1	27	28	30	21
Small town	31	29	33	33	19	34	30	30	31	31	13	33	26	32	33
Farm	24	28	20	24	20	13	25	32	18	12	85	23	26	21	25
No opinion	1	1	1	1	2	1	1	1	0	2	1	0	1	1	1

Residential Preference	Religion			Politics			Region				Income						Community Size				
	Protestant	Catholic	Jewish	Republican	Democrat	Independent	East	Midwest	South	West	$15,000 & over	$10,000-$14,999	$7,000-$9,999	$5,000-$6,999	$3,000-$4,999	Under $3,000	1,000,000 & over	500,000-999,999	50,000-499,999	2,500-49,999	Under 2,500, Rural
City	14	23	I/D	17	21	15	25	18	13	16	18	14	19	18	20	20	29	26	29	9	2
Suburban area	23	32	I/D	28	26	24	33	24	19	27	34	34	26	24	18	19	39	35	26	17	16
Small town	33	30	I/D	30	33	29	27	27	36	38	30	29	33	31	33	33	22	25	31	61	25
Farm	29	14	I/D	24	19	31	14	30	31	19	17	22	22	25	29	27	8	13	13	13	56
No opinion	1	1	I/D	1	1	1	1	1	1	0	1	1	0	2	0	1	2	1	1	0	1

I/D = Insufficient data.

Source: The Gallup Opinion Index, Political, Social and Economic Trends, Report No. 57 (Princeton, N.J.: Gallup International, March 1970), p. 21.

city people preferred small town or farm living to
their own residences than the converse. It is pertinent to note that nonwhites not only had a relatively low preference for small towns and farms,
but also a higher preference for the suburbs than
the cities; that they have not been able to fulfill
their preferences in greater degree is, of course,
a consequence of the related factors of adverse
economic circumstances and discrimination. It also
is noteworthy that the farm and small town together
found particular favor in the South, though the
West had the highest preference for the small town.
The East had a relatively high preference for both
the city and the suburbs. Finally, although there
is some tendency for income to be inversely related
to preference for farm living, the clearest influence of income is on preference for the suburbs,
with the over-$15,000 group choosing them at almost
twice the rate of the under-$3,000 group. Again it
is of interest to note that nonwhites' preferences
for the suburbs (31 percent) correspond much more
closely to the over-$15,000 income group (34 per-
cent) than to the lower income groups (18 percent
and 19 percent, respectively) of which they are
more likely to be a part.

While the insights to be gained from this survey are valuable, it is unfortunate that the nature
of the questions has created significant ambigu-
ities. Most people, for example, probably can dis-
tinguish more clearly between cities and their suburban areas than they can the borderline--whatever
it may be--between small towns and cities. In the
context of this book, in other words, it is not
clear whether an intermediate-sized city would be
considered a city or a small town by most respondents. Moreover the notion of a small town may
vary greatly. There is considerable difference if
one is choosing a small town within easy commuting
distance of a larger city or a small town in relative isolation from metropolitan areas. It seems
probable that the metropolitan resident who names
the small-town residential preference has the former
alternative in mind rather than the latter; the
latter, though, may appeal more to the person

actually residing in a small town or rural area.
The question of trend in preferences must also be
interpreted with caution over a period as short as
four years, especially when one considers the dis-
orders that occurred in many large cities during
the late 1960s.

Another difficulty with the Gallup survey is
the ambiguity of the term "preference" in the question posed to the respondents. It will be recalled
that in the French surveys it was specified that
preferences were to be established on the assumption that the respondents would be able to command
the same resources in another place that they command where they now live and work. In the Gallup
case it is impossible to know whether the respondents chose their preferred place of residence assuming their present job opportunities and income,
or whether they acted on other assumptions or even
pure fantasy. These are matters upon which one can
only speculate.

Some more explicit data are available from the
1966-67 labor mobility demonstration projects discussed in the preceding chapter. The data in Table
20 show preferred places of residence as expressed
by potential movers in prelocation interviews.
Thirty-eight percent of the respondents preferred
to relocate within their own state, but 32 percent
had no preference. The remainder expressed a broad
regional preference, which may have included the
same state in which they lived. While these data
indicate that the potential relocatees were largely
flexible with regard to receiving areas, it is probably more revealing to see how persons who actually
moved adjusted to their new environment and how
such adjustment was related to city size.

The data in Table 21 show the proportion of relocatees reporting improved housing, community facilities, and transportation, by city size. In
each case the response pattern tends to have an in-
verted U shape; that is, the proportion of relocatees
reporting improved conditions increases with city
size up to a point but then declines with increasing
size. Housing has a peak in the 50,000-99,999
range, while community facilities and transportation

TABLE 20

Location Preferences as Expressed in
Pre-Relocation Interviews, 1966-67
Labor Mobility Projects

Location Preference	Number Willing to Move	Number Actually Moving and Taking Job	Percent Satisfied with Move
Same state	3,169 (38%)	1,321	81
Specified region	2,469 (30%)	952	79.3
New England	377	178	80
Middle Atlantic	245	84	78
East North Central	716	266	86
West North Central	69	33	83
South Atlantic	424	169	81
East South Central	48	11	75
West South Central	62	18	67
Mountain	182	76	85
Pacific	346	117	79
No preference	2,695 (32%)	1,078	83

Source: Manpower Administration, U.S. Department of Labor.

each has a peak in the 100,000-249,999 range. In general the relocatees who moved to cities of between 50,000 and 500,000 seemed the most satisfied, although those who moved to cities with more than 1 million inhabitants were more satisfied with community facilities and transportation, and about equally satisfied with housing, than those who went to small towns with fewer than 10,000 inhabitants. Thus the limited evidence suggests that there is a preference for intermediate-sized cities. And if "intermediate" in this case means a place that is still not very big, there is, nevertheless, little to support the case for towns with fewer than 10,000 inhabitants.

TABLE 21

Percentage of Pilot Demonstration Project
Relocatees Reporting Improved Housing,
Community Facilities, and Transportation,
by City Size

Category	Population of Receiving City						
	Under 10,000	10,000- 49,999	50,000- 99,999	100,000- 249,999	250,000- 499,999	500,000- 999,999	1,000,000 and Over
Housing quality	40	36	45	44	39	35	38
Community facilities	42	56	59	60	58	47	49
Transportation	24	32	37	46	43	29	34

Source: Compiled from data supplied by the
U.S. Department of Labor.

THE PRESENT STUDIES: THE
CONCEPTUAL RATIONALE

Despite certain similarities the location
preference studies that are discussed in the next
chapter were conceived within a different context
from the French and American studies just discussed,
in that they were formulated and carried out with a
definite regard for regional policy considerations.
They are not as ambitious with respect either to
sampling the entire nation or to the number and
kinds of questions involved, but rather they deal
with economically lagging areas and with respondents
who were for the most part high school seniors.

One of the principal arguments presented in
Chapter 1 is that more emphasis should be given to
the development of opportunities in growing
intermediate-sized cities for persons from lagging

areas, and that comprehensive relocation assistance
should be made available to those who wish to take
advantage of these opportunities. A considerable
amount of research on growth-center theory and policy indicates that it is very often inefficient and
ineffective to try to induce growth in lagging regions with relatively few external economies. This
raises the question of whether, and under what conditions, people in lagging areas would be willing
to move to take advantage of better economic opportunities. There also are questions about the
places to which movers would prefer to go and the
extent to which expected and preferred places of
future residence correspond.

There is still a widespread belief that most
people in minority subcultures in lagging areas are
so strongly attached to their societies that they
really do not want to live in the larger society,
unless perhaps forced to do so by economic circumstances. This position is frequently encountered
among both the conservative leadership in the
places in question and among liberals who foster a
romantic notion of the pristine folk living by
values superior to those of urban-industrial society.
It is almost axiomatic with place-oriented elected
public officials that something is wrong if their
constituency is eroded by outmigration. It is also
interesting to note how quickly officials in regional development agencies may succumb to the assumption that the people in the places they are
trying to develop must feel attached to these places.

Of course the evidence is clear that there is
substantial outmigration of Mexican Americans from
south Texas, of mountaineers from central Appalachia, of blacks from Mississippi, of Indians from
the reservations. But again there is a widespread
belief that the outmigrants do not really want to
leave, that they are driven out by lack of opportunity at home. It is also widely believed that
much of this migration is misdirected to urban
ghettos. This is undoubtedly so, but it begs the
question of whether persons following previous migration streams to big cities really prefer this
alternative. They may actually prefer intermediate

locations, but have no one to help them get established there.

Then there is the argument that the selective nature of outmigration tends to denude lagging areas of whatever potential future leadership they may have and to leave behind a relatively old and-- should it be said--relatively ignorant population. From personal observation the author would be the first to agree that effective local leadership is the most indispensable ingredient in a regional development program with any hope for lagging areas. But entrenched ineptitude is in so great command in so many of these areas that bright young people cannot reasonably be expected to hang around in the hope of acquiring power and effecting positive social change. To be sure there are examples of outstanding grass-roots local leadership in lagging areas, but they are exceptional. In any case the argument that building rural sewer and water lines --with money that may be better spent, at least in part, to help people to live where they would prefer to be--is not a convincing one with respect to local leadership development. If the money were put into schools and other forms of human resource development, the case for building local leadership would be stronger, but these outlays may only increase mobility in the long run. (The Appalachian Regional Commission has admirably affirmed that it wishes to help the people of the region no matter where they may eventually live, but this does not extend to actually providing them with direct relocation assistance. Moreover ARC has been permitted more freedom by Congress to invest in human resource development programs than have such agencies as the Economic Development Administration.)

The problem of what to do with "the people left behind" is a real one and should appeal to the social consciousness of the nation at large. This is nevertheless a question of welfare and not of economic development, and the confusion between the two has led to no little waste of the nation's resources in terms of opportunity cost.

Whatever the merits of these positions the simple fact remains that considerable light can be

thrown on the location preferences of people simply
by asking them. In the studies presented in this
volume, preliminary interviews with representatives
of local schools and government agencies, in addition to data on previous migration paths, were used
to identify specific places that would: (1) correspond to notions of congested and intermediate
areas, and (2) be known to the respondents on the
basis either of firsthand experience or through the
experiences of others. In other words it would be
more meaningful to pose questions in the context of
specific places than in the context of more gener-
alized categories. (The emotionally laden term
"congested" would not have helped matters either.)
It was also felt that this approach would be more
meaningful than asking about preferences for a city
or a small town, as in the Gallup Poll, because it
is not clear what answer a person would give if he
preferred an intermediate-sized city. Of course,
despite the care taken to identify places that would
be relevant to the respondents, there were undoubtedly some who had no real experience or impression
concerning one or more of the alternatives; it can
only be conjectured whether they would tend to make
a random choice, simply choose to stay where they
are, or make a choice on some other basis. In any
case this problem is bound to be present in any
situation where there is lack of perfect knowledge.

A related problem is whether or not people can
always be expected to act--if and when the time
comes--in accord with their stated preferences. On
the other hand, if public policy cannot be related
to stated preferences, then it is not clear as to
what it should be related. Is it to be assumed
that the planners know the preferences of people
better than the people themselves? Or that the
planners know better what people ought to prefer?
Surely decisions based on these approaches would be
unacceptable to the great majority of people in our
society. And it is difficult to infer location
preferences from past migration trends, because
people have often made moves that do not correspond
to their preferences. This can happen either when
the decision is made by an employer or when people

move to a place because they want the immediate
help of a friend or relative; in such cases they do
not move because they actually prefer the <u>place</u>.

Yet another problem in location preference
studies is the assumptions under which people respond. The Gallup survey, for example, is based on
the assumption that the respondent could, as he was
told, "live anywhere in the United States that you
wanted." Does this mean with the same money income? Or the same real income? Or with improved
money or real income? Undoubtedly these or related
assumptions varied among respondents. The French
surveys represent an improvement because they usually specify that the respondent should assume that
he would have the same financial means ("les mêmes
ressources") elsewhere as he now has. But this as-
sumption--which no doubt was made by many respondents to the Gallup survey--is also open to criticism. It is not difficult to imagine that many
Parisians would like to maintain their same money
income and live in Brittany or Provence--just as
many New Yorkers would no doubt prefer to live up-
state or in Florida with the same money income. The
premise of equal financial means is simply too limited to reflect the range of people's preferences
under various assumptions.

In contrast, our studies make a variety of assumptions concerning relative wages among the home
area, the intermediate city, and the larger and
more distant city. The respondents also were re-
minded that there may be cost-of-living differences
among places and that noneconomic factors that may
influence them should also be considered. While
individual location preference choices are based on
a more or less complex pattern of interacting variables, we did not try to sort out and weigh the
relative importance of these variables; we do not
pretend to have the necessary psychological expertise. Although data were obtained on the influence
of friends and relatives and on expected place of
residence in the future, the emphasis is not on the
process by which preferences were formed but rather
on the preferences themselves, for it is to them
that public policy would have to be related.

The respondents were nearly all high school seniors. (The exceptions were also young persons: MDTA trainees in south Texas and high school juniors in a relatively new Indian school that had not yet had a senior class.) Budget constraints simply did not permit a sampling of the whole populations of the areas in question, though admittedly the results would have been valuable. On the other hand a good case can be made for limiting the statistical population to high school seniors. They are at a stage in life where they are compelled to make choices about their future careers and homes, so their stated preferences probably are based on a relatively high degree of reflection on possible location alternatives. Moreover these persons represent the future of their respective areas. No matter how attached older people may be to these areas, if the young people would rather be elsewhere, emphasis on development of the places as such appears to be misguided. Of course our surveys missed the cohorts who dropped out before completing high school, but it is not likely that they will provide the leadership necessary to reverse patterns of economic stagnation or decline.

Finally a word must be said about the inevitable counterargument of the rural development protagonists; namely, that if enough money were poured into the places that are of concern they would become more attractive and preference patterns would be altered in their favor. Surely this argument is correct if one is committed simply to force-feeding the development of places that are essentially unattractive to the mainstream of twentieth-century economic activity. Perhaps it is best to refrain from dwelling again on the economist's concept of opportunity cost, which focuses decision-making on the alternative choices that one has with regard to the use of scarce resources, including those devoted to regional development. At a minimum, however, it would seem reasonable from a social point of view to divert some part of the funds now being spent to promote regional development toward comprehensive relocation assistance for people who want to move from poor regions. The question is

not so much one of opposing regional development
assistance as favoring a more varied mix of policies to help people in areas characterized by high
unemployment or low income. The nature of the
places and people chosen for study will now be
briefly considered with these issues in mind.

THE PRESENT STUDIES: THE
PEOPLE AND PLACES

The first of our studies of location preferences under differing wage rate assumptions was
carried out in the spring of 1969 in eastern Kentucky's Big Sandy region (see Chapter 1). All of
the 625 respondents were high school seniors. A
total of seven high schools were included, the number of respondents from each ranging from 60 in
Paintsville High School to 164 in Johnson Central
High School. Females slightly outnumbered males
(328 to 297) and somewhat over 50 percent of the
seniors indicated they were going on to college
(326 to 299). On the basis of preliminary interviews, northern metropolitan areas were selected as
relevant big cities. (The term "congested city"
was used in our conceptual scheme but it was not
used in the questionnaires, because its emotive
connotation might have biased some responses.) It
was suggested verbally that Detroit and Chicago
were examples of such cities. The intermediate
cities were Lexington and Louisville, both in Kentucky but outside of Appalachia.
The last of our surveys was also made in the
Big Sandy region, where a corresponding group of
seniors was surveyed in the spring of 1971. The
repeat study was carried out for two principal reasons. First we wanted to see if the large-scale
and well-publicized development efforts in the area
were having any significant effect on location
preferences. In addition it was thought useful to
ask some questions not included in the earlier survey. Thus, although in the second survey the preferred alternatives were selected as in the first
survey, they were also selected again on the

assumption of a government relocation assistance
program. The second survey also included questions
that enabled the responses to be analyzed in terms
of those respondents who had lived outside of eastern Kentucky before and those who had not. The
responses could also be analyzed in terms of different kinds of post-high school education expectations: four-year college, junior college, vocational training, or no further education. In the
second survey the number of respondents ranged from
35 in the case of Paintsville High School to 175 in
the case of Johnson Central High School. Fifty-six
percent were female and about 25 percent had lived
at one time outside of eastern Kentucky. Thirty-
four percent intended to go on to a four-year college, 14 percent to a junior college, and 4 percent
to vocational school; 48 percent did not intend to
continue their formal education or training.

The Mexican Americans are the second largest
minority group in the United States, yet outside of
the Southwest there has been little awareness of
and even less knowledge about them. Despite recent
increasing ferment and militancy within the Mexican
American community to improve social and economic
conditions while preserving traditional values, a
recent study points out that

> It is a staggering task, for the com-
> munity has few resources.
> The average Chicano is poor. His
> median income--$5,488 in November,
> 1969, the 1970 census month--is less
> than 70% of the United States median.
> His unemployment rate almost doubles
> the national figure. Chicanos own 1%
> of the nation's businesses (all small)
> and three of its 13,500 commercial
> banks (1 small). Unlike the black
> community, Chicanos have no substan-
> tial middle or upper classes. To an
> overwhelming degree, they are un-
> skilled workers, a crippling handicap
> in an increasingly professional- and
> business-minded society.

> The Chicano is undereducated.
> Adults over 35 average 7.3 years of
> schooling compared with 12 years for
> the general population. In Texas,
> only one out of every five Chicano
> children who enters school stays
> long enough to get a high school
> diploma. One out of every five of
> his elders never attended school
> at all.[12]

By almost any standard the Mexican Americans
in Texas--and particularly in south Texas--are
worse off than Mexican Americans in the Southwest
as a whole. In 1959, 22.0 percent of Anglo and 7.3
percent of Spanish-surname urban families in the
Southwest had incomes of over $10,000; in Texas
only 3.0 percent of the Spanish-surname population
had such incomes. Median income per person in
Spanish-surname families in 1959 was only 47.3 percent of the Anglo figure; in Texas the comparable
value was only 35.5 percent, the lowest of any
southwestern state. Median income of Spanish-
surname urban males in the Southwest in 1959 was
61 percent of the Anglo figure, but in Texas the
corresponding value was only 50 percent, by far the
lowest in the region.[13]   Because Spanish-surnamed
males hold the poorer jobs in all major occupational
categories in Texas, they earn less than Anglos in
each occupation. Thus a major study of the Mexican
Americans indicates that

> it is not astonishing to find that
> relative occupational earnings of
> Mexican Americans were much lower in
> Texas than in California. However,
> the earnings ratios (Spanish-surname
> to Anglo) for San Antonio are somewhat
> larger than for all of Texas. The
> difference suggests that the poor ex-
> perience in the state as a whole is
> partly the result of the concentration
> of this ethnic population in South
> Texas, where wages are lower than in

the rest of the state. But even in
San Antonio, the largest metropolitan
area in South Texas, earnings ratios
of Mexican Americans are lower than in
California.[14]

Similarly, in relation to Anglos, "Mexican Americans
in Texas have a comparatively low participation
rates regardless of sex. The low rate is probably
related to the poor employment prospects of Spanish-
surname people in the state's underdeveloped southern region."[15]

Before deciding on who would be interviewed in
south Texas for our purposes, and the exact nature
of the questions to be posed, the author met with
government and school officials in the region to
establish what places would have relevance to such
interviews. There was a clear consensus that Mexican Americans in south Texas are very attached to
their area and that few would be likely to want to
leave, even when moving would improve their economic
opportunities. This was held to be true even for
high school juniors and seniors, plus young adults
who wanted to leave the migrant farm labor stream
for employment in a fixed place. Nevertheless it
was decided to interview persons in these two categories, since they would be among those with at
least relatively high-mobility potential.

To find relevant urban alternatives for the
south Texas Mexican Americans was not as easy as in
the other cases. In particular the preliminary
interviews pointed up differences between the Laredo
area and the lower Rio Grande valley (hereinafter
termed the Valley). It was generally felt that
Laredo area residents were relatively more mobile.
There was nearly universal agreement that potential
migration destinations for Valley residents were
limited largely to Texas, with San Antonio and
Corpus Christi being relevant cities that are intermediate in size and location--in comparison with
the large metropolitan areas of Dallas and Houston,
farther to the north. On the other hand it was
felt that Chicago (and, to a lesser extent, Detroit)
was familiar to most potential interviewees in

Laredo and that San Antonio, Corpus Christi, Dallas, and Houston all represented intermediate centers in relation to Chicago. These opinions formed the basis for the location alternatives listed on the interview schedules.

The interviews were made during the summer of 1970. High school juniors and seniors in the Valley were in Neighborhood Youth Corps programs in the following cities and towns: Brownsville, Los Fresnos, San Benito, La Feria, Port Isabel, Harlingen, and Raymondville. Another group of Valley juniors and seniors who were interviewed were in the Migrant Cultural Enrichment Program in Rio Grande City.

Valley adult interviewees were enrolled in MDTA or Adult Basic Education programs in Edinburg, Penitas, Mercedes, and Weslaco. Another group was enrolled in the Communications Skill Center of the Texas State Technical Institute in Harlingen. The vast majority of these persons were in their twenties or early thirties.

In Laredo the high school interviewees were in the Migrant Cultural Enrichment Program and the adults were taking MDTA training.

In all, 1,043 persons were interviewed. They consisted of 347 Valley adults, 463 Valley high school students, 31 Laredo adults, and 207 Laredo high school students.

In a message to Congress on July 8, 1970, the President pointed out that "The first Americans-- the Indians--are the most deprived and isolated minority group in our nation. On virtually every scale of measurement--employment, income, education, health--the condition of the Indian people ranks at the bottom."[16] The considerable publicity that has been given recently to the plight of the Indians has been accompanied by a rising tide of sentiment in favor of efforts to attract industry to the reservations. The widespread assumption that Indians are not suited to life off the reservations was reinforced by the failure of the relocation policy of the 1950s, which moved a large number of Indians directly from reservations to cities without adequate preparation and training, and which tended explicitly or implicitly to denigrate the Indians'

own culture.[17] Thus a recent study asserts that
"if this book proves anything, it is that Indian
societies are still vital, and that Indian people
desire and intend to maintain them."[18] In fact
most Indian leaders do favor economic development
on the reservations. "It would be fair to say,"
writes a prominent Indian spokesman, "that of any
agency in the government in the last few years EDA
has been the most responsive to tribal programs."[19]
He would even transfer the Bureau of Indian Affairs
"not to Health, Education and Welfare, but to Commerce. Since the bureau would be primarily a grant-
ing and technical assistance agency, it would need
to be in a department where economic development
was the primary mission. It could then become
merged with the Economic Development Administration
in a special Indian section. . . ."[20]

Similarly a U.S. Department of Labor report to
the Joint Economic Committee of Congress states that:

> planning of MDTA [Manpower Develop-
> ment and Training Act] training
> should be coordinated very closely
> with planning for industrial develop-
> ment in or near the reservations, and
> MDTA should make little or no effort
> toward training reservation Indians
> for relocation away from the reserva-
> tions unless tribal leaders specifi-
> cally request it. . . . [T]he people
> planning our programs must divest
> themselves of the discredited idea
> that the only solution for the Indian
> problem is to train them to be like
> white people and to move them into
> the large cities.[21]

Government efforts over the past decade to
bring industry to reservations have unfortunately
produced only 4,000 jobs for Indians,[22] and a high
proportion of these have gone to females.

The tribes chosen for study here--the Navaho,
Zuni, and Rio Grande Pueblos--were selected because
these peoples have managed particularly well to
reconcile what Fey and McNickle term "The divergent

views that alternatively have blessed and menaced
the record of Government-Indian relations."[23]   They
ask: "How did it happen that the Navajo tribe, the
onetime incorrigible raiders of the Southwest, managed to avoid the consequences of the 'compulsory
process' and win the right to hold fast to their
institutions? The question could be asked of the
Rio Grande Pueblos and of the Zuni . . . in the
West. Something in these people never yielded."[24]

Even though the reasons for this phenomenon are
not clear, the responses reported in this study were
obtained from Indians in tribes that have apparently
achieved accommodation with the larger society--but
without sacrificing the stability of their own tra-
ditions and values. It is not surprising, therefore, that preliminary discussions with Bureau of
Indian Affairs (BIA) and Indian officials in the
region yielded a clear consensus that the respondents probably would show a high degree of attach-
ment to their present communities.

In the preliminary interviews, Albuquerque
clearly represented the intermediate alternative.[25]
And it was felt that nearly all of the respondents
would have some impression of conditions in Chicago,
Los Angeles, or the San Francisco Bay area. Denver
was a widely mentioned potential migration destination, but while it was clearly bigger and farther
away than Albuquerque, it was also intermediate in
relation to the "large city" alternatives. For
this reason, locational preferences under different
relative wage structure assumptions were analyzed
first with the present community of residence,
Albuquerque, Chicago, Los Angeles, and the San
Francisco Bay area as location alternatives. It
was then done with the present community of residence, Albuquerque, and Denver as the alternatives.

The survey questionnaires were administered
under the supervision of the author in December
1970. Of the 560 respondents, 322 were Navahos,
59 were Zunis, 110 were from the Southern Pueblos,
and 69 from the Northern Pueblos.* Males and

_____

*The Northern Pueblo schools were Espanola,
Taos, Pojoaque, and St. Catherine. The Southern

females were equally divided. And 89 percent of
all respondents planned to continue their education
beyond high school.

The Mississippi study was carried out in four
southwestern counties corresponding to our concept
of a lagging area. The counties--Amite, Jefferson,
Pike and Walthall--were selected because they had
roughly the same number of blacks and whites in the
schools, and because we had the help of the EDA
district office in gaining the cooperation of local
school officials. Median family income in the
four-county area in 1960 was $2,616, compared to
$2,884 in the whole of Mississippi and $5,660 in
the United States. The proportion of families with
an income of less than $3,000 in 1960 ranged from
47 percent in Pike county to 74 percent in Jefferson
county; the corresponding value for Mississippi was
52 percent and that for the United States was only
14 percent. The median years of school attended by
persons 25 and older ranged from 6.8 in Jefferson
county to 9.2 in Pike county; the state value was
8.9 and that for the nation 10.6.[26]

Population in the four counties declined over
the past decade because of heavy rates of net outmigration, especially for the black population. As
the data in Table 22 indicate, total population decline ranged from 7.5 percent in Walthall county to
11.6 percent in Amite county. Negro net outmigration was 34.6 percent in both Amite and Walthall
counties and over 20 percent in the other two
counties.

There were a total of 1,421 respondents to the
Mississippi questionnaire. They were attending
high schools in the six school districts of the
four counties just discussed, as well as two junior
colleges, three Manpower Development and Training

Pueblo schools were Jemez Valley, Bernalillo, and
Laguna-Acoma. Zuni had one high school. Two Navaho
schools were included, Fort Wingate and Many Farms.
The last had no senior class yet, so juniors were
included instead.

TABLE 22

Estimates of Components of Change for the Total Population and
for Negroes, 1960 to 1970, in Amite, Jefferson, Pike,
and Walthall Counties, Mississippi

| Category | Population | | Change, 1960-70 | | Components of Change | | | |
	April 1, 1960	April 1, 1970	Number	Percent	Births	Deaths	Net Migration Number	Net Migration Percent
Amite	15,573	13,763	-1,810	-11.6	3,098	1,492	-3,416	-21.9
Negroes	8,443	6,949	-1,494	-17.7	2,175	745	-2,924	-34.6
Jefferson	10,142	9,295	-847	-8.4	2,181	1,290	-1,738	-17.1
Negroes	7,653	6,999	-654	-8.5	1,885	895	-1,644	-21.5
Pike	35,063	31,756	-3,307	-9.4	7,118	4,102	-6,323	-18.0
Negroes	15,408	13,853	-1,555	-10.1	3,924	1,810	-3,669	-23.8
Walthall	13,512	12,500	-1,012	-7.5	2,761	1,320	-2,453	-18.2
Negroes	6,100	5,097	-1,003	-16.4	1,665	559	-2,109	-34.6

Source: "Population Estimates and Projections: Components of Population Change by County, 1960 to 1970," Current Population Reports, Series P-25, No. 461 (June 28, 1971), pp. 36-38.

Act centers, and four academies located in or near
the four counties. Although not all of the respondents were residents of these counties, they were
from southwestern Mississippi. Of the total, 54
percent were male and 46 percent female. Fifty-one
percent of the respondents were white and 49 percent were black. Seniors in public high schools
accounted for 60 percent of the total, junior colleges for 26 percent, MDTA centers for 10 percent,
and private academies for 3 percent.

Preliminary interviews in the area suggested
that Chicago, Detroit, Houston, and Los Angeles
were relevant "congested" areas, and that Jackson,
Memphis, and Baton Rouge were relevant intermediate
centers. New Orleans is fairly close to the counties in question, but it was omitted from the questionnaire because it did not fit clearly into either
the congested or intermediate categories. The survey was administered in November 1970.

4

THE CASE STUDIES

INTRODUCTION

Location preferences of the people and places
just described are analyzed in this chapter within
an essentially common framework. In particular the
eight different relative wage structures shown in
Table 23 were given to all respondents. The three
wages assumed in each instance correspond, of course,
to the home community, intermediate city, and congested city alternatives, respectively. The reported results differ somewhat among the four cases
because some cross tabulations that seemed relevant
in one case may not have seemed so in another.
Also a few questions were added in later surveys on
the basis of what was learned in earlier surveys.
For example, questions related to relocation assistance were not asked in the 1969 study in eastern
Kentucky, although they were introduced in the 1971
study of the same area. (The Indians were not asked
about relocation assistance because the Bureau of
Indian Affairs already has a voluntary program to
provide comprehensive assistance to Indians moving
to selected cities.) In general, then, while each
study was carried out on its own merits, there is a
firm basis for comparative analysis.

EASTERN KENTUCKY--1969

The data in Table 23 show the location preferences of all eastern Kentucky respondents under differing wage rate assumptions. Eight different relative wage structures were given for three locations:
the student's own community, Lexington or Louisville
(both outside of Appalachia), and a northern city.

If the wage rate is higher in the eastern Kentucky community than in the other locations (Case V),
then over 80 percent of the respondents would stay
in their home town. Most of the remaining respondents would move to Lexington or Louisville, even
though they would receive $1.00 less per hour. In
Case I, where wages are equal in all locations,
about 64 percent would stay at home, but over 25
percent would go to Lexington or Louisville and 10
percent would go North.

What is particularly striking is that, in any
case where the wage in Lexington or Louisville exceeds that in the home community, more respondents
would prefer these cities to the home community.
Moreover the preference for these cities increases
consistently with the magnitude of the wage differential between the home community and the urban centers. For example, when the difference is only
$0.25 (Case II), those who would move to Lexington
or Louisville outnumber those who would stay in
eastern Kentucky by 36 percent to 25 percent. When
the wage differential is increased to $0.50 (Case
III), the ratio becomes 40 percent to 18 percent.
When the differential is increased to $0.75 (Case
IV), it becomes 36 percent to 10 percent; at a differential of $1.00 (Case VII), it becomes 35 percent
to 9 percent; and at $2.00 (CASE VIII), it is 27
percent to 6 percent.

No less striking is the disposition of the
students to avoid going to a northern city. In the
two cases where the wage in Lexington or Louisville
exceeds that in the northern city (Cases V and VI),
very few respondents would go north. In Cases II
and III, where the northern wage rate is highest,
about as many respondents would prefer to go to
Lexington or Louisville as to go north. Even in

Relative Frequency of Location Preferences of Eastern Kentucky High School Seniors for Eastern Kentucky, Lexington or Louisville, and a Northern City, by Selected Groups, 1969

Case and Location Preference	Hourly Wage ($)	All Respondents (%)	Male (%)	Female (%)	College-Bound (%)	Noncollege Bound (%)
I Eastern Kentucky	1.50	64.2	73.6	56.2	61.7	67.2
Lexington, Louisville	1.50	25.8	18.8	31.8	31.9	18.6
Northern City	1.50	10.0	7.6	12.0	6.4	14.2
II Eastern Kentucky	1.50	25.1	31.2	19.7	19.7	31.4
Lexington, Louisville	1.75	35.8	32.4	38.7	40.8	29.8
Northern City	2.00	39.1	36.4	41.6	39.4	38.8
III Eastern Kentucky	1.50	18.0	21.6	15.0	14.9	21.6
Lexington, Louisville	2.00	39.6	36.9	41.8	45.4	32.9
Northern City	2.50	42.4	41.5	43.2	39.7	45.5
IV Eastern Kentucky	1.50	9.7	8.4	11.0	7.0	12.9
Lexington, Louisville	2.25	36.5	37.3	35.7	40.6	31.6
Northern City	3.00	53.8	54.3	53.3	52.4	55.5
V Eastern Kentucky	3.50	81.3	86.5	76.6	79.8	83.1
Lexington, Louisville	2.50	13.4	10.4	16.1	15.8	10.5
Northern City	1.50	5.3	3.1	7.3	4.4	6.4
VI Eastern Kentucky	1.50	10.0	9.1	10.8	6.6	14.3
Lexington, Louisville	3.50	81.1	84.2	78.3	87.1	72.6
Northern City	2.50	8.9	6.6	10.8	6.3	12.1
VII Eastern Kentucky	1.50	8.7	7.3	10.0	6.6	11.3
Lexington, Louisville	2.50	34.9	34.2	35.6	38.1	30.9
Northern City	3.50	56.4	58.5	54.4	55.3	57.8
VIII Eastern Kentucky	1.50	6.5	4.0	8.8	3.6	10.0
Lexington, Louisville	3.50	27.1	26.7	27.4	31.4	21.7
Northern City	5.50	66.5	69.2	63.8	65.0	68.3

Note: Individual percentages do not always add to 100 because of rounding.

Case VII, 35 percent would move to Lexington or
Louisville even though they could make $1.00 more
in the North; in Case VIII, 27 percent would move
to the Kentucky urban centers even though they could
make $2.00 more in the North.

Table 23 also breaks down locational preferences by male and female groups. Where the wage
spread is relatively wide, the groups have similar
patterns. When the wage rate is equal in all locations (Case I), there is a much stronger tendency
for females to leave eastern Kentucky, with a great
majority of the migrants preferring Lexington or
Louisville to a northern city. As the wage spread
becomes wider to the detriment of eastern Kentucky,
both males and females increasingly prefer to leave
eastern Kentucky. That both groups clearly prefer
Lexington or Louisville to a northern city is seen
by comparing Cases VI and VII, where the wage rates
in Lexington and Louisville are reversed from that
in the North, with eastern Kentucky held constant.

The data on preferences by college-bound (CB)
and noncollege-bound (NCB) students (Table 23) show
that CB students are less attached to eastern Kentucky than NCB students. They also indicate that
CB students leaving eastern Kentucky have a relatively greater preference for Lexington or Louisville than do NCB students, who are more inclined
to move to industrial centers in the North. For
example, even when wage rates are equal in all locations (Case I), 31.9 percent of the CB students
would still prefer Lexington or Louisville; in the
case where the Lexington-Louisville wage is highest
(Case VI), 87.1 percent of the CB students prefer
these cities.

In the regression equations shown in Table 24,
the proportion of students preferring to remain in
a given location is related to the opportunity cost
of remaining. An opportunity cost unit is here defined by

$$\frac{\text{wage in given location - wage in best alternative location}}{25}$$

TABLE 24

Regressions Relating Opportunity Cost (X) to Percentage of Students,
by Selected Groups, Preferring a Given Location (Y), 1969

Group	Location Preference	Regression Equation	R^2	Beta Coefficient	t
All students	Eastern Kentucky	Y=47.5+3.89X (1.07)	.687	.82	3.63
	Lexington, Louisville	Y=46.1+4.15X (1.58)	.534	.73	2.62
	Northern city	Y=31.8+4.46X (0.82)	.830	.91	5.41
College-bound students	Eastern Kentucky	Y=45.0+3.95X (1.12)	.675	.82	3.53
	Lexington, Louisville	Y=51.4+4.39X (1.68)	.557	.75	2.76
	Northern city	Y=30.0+4.78X (0.92)	.799	.89	4.88
Noncollege-bound students	Eastern Kentucky	Y=50.9+3.90X (1.03)	.705	.84	3.78
	Lexington, Louisville	Y=40.1+3.82X (1.55)	.505	.71	2.47
	Northern city	Y=33.9+4.45X (0.77)	.848	.92	8.79
Male students	Eastern Kentucky	Y=53.1+4.56X (1.10)	.722	.85	3.95
	Lexington, Louisville	Y=44.4+4.18X (1.91)	.443	.67	2.18
	Northern city	Y=31.0+4.78X (0.91)	.818	.90	5.20
College-bound males	Eastern Kentucky	Y=50.7+4.46X (1.18)	.704	.84	3.78
	Lexington, Louisville	Y=50.0+3.93X (2.00)	.392	.63	1.97
	Northern city	Y=27.4+4.27X (0.83)	.814	.90	5.13
Noncollege-bound males	Eastern Kentucky	Y=55.7+4.59X (1.12)	.737	.86	4.10
	Lexington, Louisville	Y=37.3+4.65X (1.85)	.512	.72	2.51
	Northern city	Y=36.3+5.44X (1.04)	.821	.91	5.24
Female students	Eastern Kentucky	Y=43.2+3.42X (1.04)	.642	.80	3.29
	Lexington, Louisville	Y=43.3+4.04X (1.30)	.616	.79	3.10
	Northern city	Y=32.7+4.13X (0.79)	.822	.91	5.26
College-bound females	Eastern Kentucky	Y=39.2+3.46X (1.09)	.627	.79	3.17
	Lexington, Louisville	Y=52.6+4.89X (1.29)	.707	.84	3.81
	Northern city	Y=33.3+4.62X (1.02)	.772	.88	4.51
Noncollege-bound females	Eastern Kentucky	Y=47.7+3.39X (0.98)	.664	.81	3.44
	Lexington, Louisville	Y=41.7+3.13X (1.40)	.452	.67	2.23
	Northern city	Y=32.3+3.58X (0.54)	.876	.94	6.50

Note: Numbers in parentheses are standard errors.

Thus the opportunity cost of remaining in eastern Kentucky is 0 in Case I, -2 in Case II, -4 in Case III, -6 in Case IV, and so forth. Similarly the opportunity cost of remaining in a northern city is -8 in Case V, -4 in Case VI, +4 in Case VII, and +8 in Case VIII.

For all students and for each selected group of students, the degree of responsiveness to opportunity cost is high; in only three equations is R^2 less than .50. The degree of responsiveness, or goodness of fit for each group, is highest when the opportunity cost of living in a northern city is considered. Degree of responsiveness is lowest when considered from the perspective of Lexington or Louisville.

Although the students are generally responsive to wage differences, they are also influenced in their choice of location by where their friends and relatives have gone. The data show that about 50 percent of the students are influenced by this factor. For males the percentage is 47; for females it is 50. It is particularly noteworthy that 62 percent of the NCB students are influenced by friends and relatives who have migrated, whereas this is the case for only 37 percent of the CB students. The difference is probably a reflection of the more immediate need of NCB students for help in migration; the CB students can defer specific decisions in this regard and college experiences will also give them more information on which to act.* These considerations for eastern Kentucky may also explain why the regression equation with the best fit in Table 24 is that for NCB males.

In addition to analyzing preference patterns under various hypothetical conditions, it is

---

*Most of the CB students would not be severing regional ties by going to college. Slightly over two-thirds of the CB students indicated that they intended to go to college in eastern Kentucky. This figure includes those intending to Eastern Kentucky University, which lies just outside the region proper.

instructive to know where the respondents actually expect to live. Responses in this regard are presented in Table 25. Expectations are specified for five years in the future to allow for graduation from college by the CB students. Seventy percent of all students expect to reside outside of eastern Kentucky, with 40 percent expecting to live outside of Kentucky and 30 percent expecting to live in Lexington or Louisville. Contrary to the usually accepted belief that poor regions lose a relatively large proportion of their better-educated people, 32 percent of the CB students expect to reside in eastern Kentucky, as contrasted with only 27 percent of the NCB students. Male and NCB students are particularly inclined to either leave the state or to live in Lexington or Louisville.

TABLE 25

Expected Place of Residence in Five Years of
Eastern Kentucky High School Seniors,
by Sex and by College- and
Noncollege-Bound Groups, 1969
(percentage)

Group	Lexington or Louisville	Eastern Kentucky	Outside Kentucky
Total	30	30	40
Males	26	29	45
Females	34	31	36
College-bound	35	32	33
Noncollege-bound	25	27	48

Note: Individual percentages do not always add to 100 because of rounding.

In general these results demonstrate that even in one of the most lagging Appalachian areas, there is considerable willingness and readiness to move to areas that offer better economic opportunities. Although family considerations are still important

in influencing migration paths, especially for
those who do not go to college, there is in fact
considerable sensitivity to relative wages in location preferences and expectations. Moreover it is
erroneous to believe that outmigrants from this area
prefer to go to big metropolitan areas in the North.
There is a clear tendency to prefer intermediate
areas between the lagging rural area and the northern metropolitan areas. These findings support
policies that would divert rural outmigrants from
big cities toward intermediate areas, as well as
policies that would give potential migrants skills
and training to match job opportunities in intermediate areas, plus comprehensive relocation assistance. In the present case this would mean matching education and training programs in eastern Kentucky with the job requirements of industries in
Lexington or Louisville, where labor markets have
been tight. The question is not one of "moving out"
people; in our market system it is no more possible
to compel mountain people to leave than it is possible to compel industry to move to the mountains.
But it is a question of giving people viable alter-
natives--and thereby the opportunity for genuine
choice.

THE MEXICAN AMERICANS

The data in Table 26 show the locational preferences of the Mexican American respondents by selected groups under various wage rate assumptions.
With the wage rate the same in all locations (Case
I), over three-fourths of all respondents would
stay in south Texas. But only a relatively small
wage advantage outside south Texas (Case II) leads
to over 50 percent of the respondents preferring to
leave for larger Texas cities. As the wage differential between south Texas or Dallas or Houston increases, with the wage in San Antonio or Corpus
Christi being in between (Cases I-IV, VII, VIII),
there is a consistent shift from south Texas to the
northern Texas cities; the proportion that would go
to the intermediate cities remains relatively

TABLE 26

Relative Frequency of Location Preferences of Mexican Americans in South Texas
for South Texas, San Antonio or Corpus Christi, and Dallas or Houston,
by Selected Groups

Case and Location Preference	Hourly Wage ($)	All Respondents (%)	High School (%)	Adults (%)	Males (%)	Females (%)	Laredo (%)	Valley (%)
I South Texas	1.50	77	67	84	83	68	71	78
San Antonio, Corpus Christi	1.50	10	12	9	7	14	14	9
Dallas, Houston	1.50	13	21	7	10	18	15	13
II South Texas	1.50	47	26	64	56	34	28	53
San Antonio, Corpus Christi	1.75	13	17	11	12	16	18	12
Dallas, Houston	2.00	40	57	25	32	51	55	35
III South Texas	1.50	38	18	55	44	30	17	45
San Antonio, Corpus Christi	2.00	15	19	11	14	16	22	13
Dallas, Houston	2.50	47	63	34	42	54	61	43
IV South Texas	1.50	30	15	43	33	26	12	36
San Antonio, Corpus Christi	2.25	13	15	11	12	14	16	12
Dallas, Houston	3.00	57	70	46	55	59	72	52
V South Texas	3.50	84	77	90	88	79	82	85
San Antonio, Corpus Christi	2.50	8	11	6	7	11	9	8
Dallas, Houston	1.50	7	12	3	6	10	8	7
VI South Texas	1.50	31	17	42	33	27	13	36
San Antonio, Corpus Christi	3.50	58	65	52	56	59	71	53
Dallas, Houston	2.50	12	18	6	10	14	16	10
VII South Texas	1.50	29	16	40	31	25	10	34
San Antonio, Corpus Christi	2.50	13	15	10	11	14	17	11
Dallas, Houston	3.50	59	69	50	57	61	73	54
VIII South Texas	1.50	23	13	30	23	22	9	27
San Antonio, Corpus Christi	3.50	13	14	12	12	13	15	12
Dallas, Houston	5.50	65	73	58	66	65	76	61

constant. On the other hand a comparison of Cases
VI and VII, which reverse the wage rates in the two
sets of alternatives outside of south Texas (with
south Texas held constant), shows that there is virtually no difference in the attractive power of the
non-south Texas cities.

Compared to the totals for all respondents, it
is clear in each case that the high school students
prefer to leave south Texas much more than do the
adults. In Case II, for example, about three-
fourths of the high school students would leave
south Texas, while about two-thirds of the adults
would stay. Whether this simply reflects the usual
inverse relationship between migration and age or
whether there is also a shift over time in favor of
outmigration within age groups cannot be ascertained
from the evidence here. However the wide disparity
between these groups and the fact that most of the
adults are young suggest the possibility of a shift.

The values shown in Table 26 clearly indicate
that females prefer to leave south Texas more than
males. Only in Case VIII, where the wages outside
of south Texas depart the most from the wage in
south Texas, are the male and female patterns nearly
the same. The females are relatively more attracted
by Dallas and Houston, but a comparison of Cases VI
and VII indicates almost no difference in the attractive power of San Antonio and Corpus Christi on
the one hand and Dallas and Houston on the other.

Table 26 also presents a breakdown of preferences according to whether the respondents reside
in the Laredo area or in the Valley. There is considerable responsiveness to relative wage changes,
though the Laredo respondents are notably less attached to their area than are the Valley respondents.
This supports the opinions encountered in preliminary
interviews. Of course a bias is introduced by the
fact that the Laredo group includes a high proportion of relatively mobile high school students. But
when Laredo and Valley high school students were
compared, it was found that the Laredo students were
more mobile. Of the three cities shown in Table 26,
for example, with a wage structure as in Case IV,
21 percent of the Valley students would stay home,

but only 12 percent of the Laredo students would do
so; with a wage structure as in Case V, the comparable values are 22 percent and 9 percent respectively. It is pertinent to note that in Case VII,
where the south Texas wage is highest, 82 percent
of the Laredo students would stay home, compared to
only 75 percent of those in the Valley. In other
words Laredo students react more to money incentives,
whether they favor the home area or some other place.

The respondents shown in Table 27 refer to the
same areas as Table 26, except that Chicago and Detroit are substituted for Dallas and Houston.
These respondents were obtained from the 413 Laredo
and Valley (Rio Grande City) former migrant farm
workers, rather than from all 1,043 respondents.
Therefore the results are not strictly comparable
to those given in Table 26. Nevertheless there is
a striking contrast between the number of persons
who would leave south Texas and the number of persons who would go to intermediate cities (San Antonio or Corpus Christi) rather than large northern
metropolitan areas. In Table 27 it is seen that in
every case (except in Case V, where the relative
frequencies are the same), a higher proportion
would prefer to leave south Texas than in Table 26.
However there is now a definite tendency to prefer
the intermediate Texas cities. In Case VII, for example, the northern city ($3.50) is preferred by 43
percent and San Antonio or Corpus Christi ($2.50)
by 37 percent. With these rates reversed and that
in south Texas held constant ($1.50), the northern
city is preferred by only 4 percent, whereas San
Antonio or Corpus Christi is preferred by 76 percent. (It will be recalled that reversing these
rates in Table 26 showed that apparently the respondents were indifferent as to choosing between
San Antonio and Corpus Christi on the one hand and
Dallas and Houston on the other. This was also
true for the various subgroups.) The marked preference for the Texas cities also shows up in the
various subgroups, as seen in Table 27.

In general the results indicate that under
present conditions the migration potential of high
school graduates and many younger adults is greater

TABLE 27

Relative Frequency of Location Preferences of Mexican Americans in South Texas for South Texas, San Antonio or Corpus Christi, and Chicago or Detroit, by Selected Groups

Case and Location Preference	Hourly Wage ($)	All Respondents (%)	High School (%)	Adults (%)	Males (%)	Females (%)	Laredo (%)	Valley (%)
I South Texas	1.50	75	72	79	82	68	73	78
San Antonio, Corpus Christi	1.50	15	16	14	12	18	15	14
Chicago, Detroit	1.50	10	12	8	6	14	11	9
II South Texas	1.50	42	36	48	52	31	37	48
San Antonio, Corpus Christi	1.75	23	23	23	20	25	25	20
Chicago, Detroit	2.00	35	41	29	27	43	38	32
III South Texas	1.50	31	24	37	37	25	25	38
San Antonio, Corpus Christi	2.00	34	37	32	37	32	38	29
Chicago, Detroit	2.50	35	39	31	27	43	36	33
IV South Texas	1.50	21	16	27	24	19	17	28
San Antonio, Corpus Christi	2.25	38	36	40	41	35	38	37
Chicago, Detroit	3.00	41	48	34	35	47	45	36
V South Texas	3.50	84	87	81	86	81	86	81
San Antonio, Corpus Christi	2.50	11	9	13	9	13	10	13
Chicago, Detroit	1.50	5	5	5	4	6	4	6
VI South Texas	1.50	20	15	25	24	16	16	25
San Antonio, Corpus Christi	3.50	76	80	72	73	79	80	71
Chicago, Detroit	2.50	4	5	3	3	5	5	3
VII South Texas	1.50	20	14	27	22	18	15	28
San Antonio, Corpus Christi	2.50	37	37	37	42	32	39	34
Chicago, Detroit	3.50	43	49	37	36	50	46	38
VIII South Texas	1.50	14	11	16	14	13	12	16
San Antonio, Corpus Christi	3.50	30	32	28	33	27	34	25
Chicago, Detroit	5.50	56	57	56	53	59	54	60

than is generally believed or admitted. On the
basis of preliminary interviews it was hypothesized
that those Mexican Americans who would prefer to
migrate would prefer San Antonio or Corpus Christi
over Dallas or Houston. However the data indicate
that all of these Texas cities have approximately
equal attractiveness to potential migrants. In contrast it is quite clear that the Texas cities are
preferred to Chicago or Detroit.

The high school students and the Laredo adults
were asked, "If there were a government program to
pay your moving expenses, find you a job, help find
you a place to live and help to get you settled,
how much more willing than you are now would you be
to leave your home town?" Of the 701 respondents,
45 percent said they would be a lot more willing
and 35 percent stated they would be moderately more
willing. None of the comparable percentages for
the various subgroups varied by more than three percentage points from these values. The data in Tables
28 and 29 also show that many more persons would prefer to leave south Texas if there were a government
program to assist in relocation. A comparison of
Cases II and V in Table 28 shows that such a program
would increase the number and proportion of migrants
who would go to the intermediate growth cities (com-
pare these cases with Cases VI and VII in Table 26).

In Table 29 Chicago and Detroit replace Dallas
and Houston. Here the introduction of government
relocation assistance does not have the same degree
of influence on rechanneling migration paths. Nevertheless in comparing Case I in Table 27 with Case
I in Table 29, and Case V in Table 27 with the corresponding Case IV in Table 29, it is evident that relocation assistance would increase outmigration--
and would do so in favor of San Antonio and Corpus
Christi.

The respondents were also asked, "If you would
leave the town where you live now, would your decision where to go be influenced by where friends and
relatives have gone?" Of all persons responding,
47 percent replied in the affirmative. Of this
group, 31 percent indicated that the influence of
family and friends would be weak; the remainder felt
it would be either moderate (43 percent) or strong
(26 percent).

TABLE 28

Relative Frequency of Location Preferences of Mexican Americans in South Texas for South Texas, San Antonio or Corpus Christi, and Dallas or Houston, by Selected Groups--If there were a Government Relocation Aid Program

Case and Location Preference	Hourly Wage ($)	All Respondents (%)	High School (%)	Adults (%)	Males (%)	Females (%)	Laredo (%)	Valley (%)
I South Texas	1.50	57	52	62	63	50	53	62
San Antonio, Corpus Christi	1.50	19	19	19	16	21	20	17
Dallas, Houston	1.50	24	29	20	21	28	27	21
II South Texas	1.50	16	11	21	18	13	12	22
San Antonio, Corpus Christi	2.50	19	19	19	21	17	21	17
Dallas, Houston	3.50	65	70	60	61	69	68	62
III South Texas	1.50	13	10	15	14	11	11	16
San Antonio, Corpus Christi	3.50	20	23	16	22	17	24	13
Dallas, Houston	5.50	68	67	68	63	72	65	71
IV South Texas	3.50	78	75	80	84	71	76	80
San Antonio, Corpus Christi	2.50	12	12	12	9	15	13	10
Dallas, Houston	1.50	10	12	8	6	14	11	9
V South Texas	1.50	16	12	19	15	16	12	20
San Antonio, Corpus Christi	3.50	73	75	71	76	70	76	69
Dallas, Houston	2.50	12	13	10	9	14	12	11

TABLE 29

Relative Frequency of Location Preferences of Mexican Americans in South Texas for South Texas, San Antonio or Corpus Christi, and Chicago or Detroit, by Selected Group--If there were a Government Relocation Aid Program

Case and Location Preference	Hourly Wage ($)	All Respondents (%)	High School (%)	Adults (%)	Males (%)	Females (%)	Laredo (%)	Valley (%)
I South Texas	1.50	68	66	71	77	59	67	70
San Antonio, Corpus Christi	1.50	21	19	22	16	25	20	22
Chicago, Detroit	1.50	11	15	7	7	15	13	8
II South Texas	1.50	18	14	21	20	16	15	22
San Antonio, Corpus Christi	2.50	36	31	41	40	32	34	38
Chicago, Detroit	3.50	46	55	38	40	53	51	40
III South Texas	1.50	13	11	15	13	13	11	16
San Antonio, Corpus Christi	3.50	30	29	32	32	29	31	29
Chicago, Detroit	5.50	57	60	53	55	58	58	55.
IV South Texas	3.50	79	76	83	86	73	77	83
San Antonio, Corpus Christi	2.50	14	17	11	10	19	17	10
Chicago, Detroit	1.50	6	7	6	4	8	6	7
V South Texas	1.50	17	15	19	19	15	15	20
San Antonio, Corpus Christi	3.50	77	78	75	77	77	79	73
Chicago, Detroit	2.50	6	7	5	4	8	6	6

Expected place of residence for all respondents and each subgroup is shown in Table 30. More than 50 percent of all respondents expect to live outside of south Texas. The proportion of persons in high school who expect to reside outside of the region is particularly large, whereas the adult group shows the greatest expectations of remaining. About 25 percent of all respondents expect to live in places other than south Texas or the four Texas cities in question. Despite past tendencies for many Mexican Americans from south Texas to move to California, only 3.6 percent of all respondents indicated that they expected to live there in five years.

TABLE 30

Expected Place of Residence in Five Years:
Mexican Americans in South Texas,
by Selected Groups

| Group | Proportion Expecting to Live in | | | |
	South Texas	San Antonio or Corpus Christi	Dallas or Houston	Elsewhere
All re- spondents	47	11	17	26
High school	34	13	21	32
Adults	58	9	13	20
Males	52	9	15	23
Females	39	13	19	29
Laredo	38	16	20	26
Valley	49	9	16	26

Finally the regression equations in Table 31 show the proportion of respondents preferring to remain in south Texas as a function of the opportunity cost of staying (which is defined as in the eastern Kentucky case). The data refer only to the options presented in Tables 26 and 28. It is clear that there is a high degree of responsiveness to

TABLE 31

Regressions Relating Opportunity Cost (X) to Percentage of Respondents
Preferring to Remain in South Texas (Y), by Selected Groups

Group	Without Relocation Assistance		With Relocation Assistance	
	Regression Equation	R^2	Regression Equation	R^2
All respondents	Y=61.6+3.35X	.763	Y=55.7+3.52X	.852
High school	Y=48.1+3.39X	.637	Y=51.6+3.50X	.835
Adults	Y=72.8+3.35X	.871	Y=59.3+3.55X	.873
Males	Y=67.3+3.68X	.811	Y=60.3+3.84X	.846
Females	Y=53.7+2.96X	.673	Y=50.1+3.20X	.856
Laredo	Y=50.1+3.96X	.668	Y=52.5+3.51X	.830
Valley	Y=65.2+3.19X	.809	Y=59.5+3.49X	.874

Note: The equations (both sets) refer to San Antonio or Corpus Christi, and Dallas or Houston, as the alternatives to south Texas. The data for the regressions were taken from Tables 26 and 28.

opportunity cost. Moreover with the exception of
the Laredo group, the regression coefficient for
every group is higher with relocation assistance
than without it, indicating that there would be
greater responsiveness to opportunity cost if relocation assistance were made available.

To summarize, remoteness from the major centers
of the nation, poor resources, underdeveloped human
resources and pressures from Mexico have combined to
make south Texas one of the country's poorest regions, and one where solutions seem the most difficult. Although government policy has designated
"growth centers" within south Texas, such centers
do not have sufficient external economies to significantly improve the economic opportunities available in the region.

In contrast to the reluctance of firms to move
into south Texas, there is considerable willingness,
at least on the part of younger persons, to leave
the region to take advantage of economic and other
opportunities elsewhere. The evidence indicates
that a government program to assist those who choose
to move would increase outmigration from the region,
and that it might redirect some migration into San
Antonio and Corpus Christi from other standard
metropolitan statistical areas (SMSAs). Such a
program could be of particular benefit to females,
in that females express a greater desire to leave
the area than males do. Nevertheless Social Security sample data indicate that about 75 percent of
the outmigrants from south Texas are males.

The Mexican Americans responding to the survey
on locational preferences tended to prefer Texas
cities to Chicago or Detroit, but they did not show
any particular preference either for San Antonio
and Corpus Christi on the one hand or for Dallas
and Houston on the other. In any event, Corpus
Christi and especially San Antonio seem to be the
most feasible centers for aiding the people of
south Texas. They are closer to the region than
Houston or Dallas, and they probably have fewer diseconomies. San Antonio exerts an influence over a
large part of south Texas, and evidence indicates
that, in relation to other rural urban migrants,

Mexican American migrants from south Texas to San
Antonio are particularly well-adjusted and satisfied.[1]

The findings suggest that comprehensive relocation assistance would be more efficient in increasing income and employment opportunities for Mexican
Americans in south Texas than would be efforts to
attract industry to the region. Of course we are
talking in marginal terms and not of whole populations; for the people remaining in south Texas, the
lack of jobs is obviously an important issue. But
so long as the relative disadvantages of the region
persist, chasing smokestacks is no substitute for
manpower and human resource development programs to
increase mobility potentials.

THE INDIANS

The data in Table 32 show the locational preferences of all respondents using the Chicago, Los
Angeles, and San Francisco Bay large-city alternatives. Response patterns also are shown for the
Navaho, Zuni, Northern Pueblo, and Southern Pueblo
groups, as well as for males and females and for
those who expect to continue their education beyond
high school (in contrast to those who do not).

It is striking that with the wage rate the same
in all places (Case I), well over 50 percent of the
respondents would leave, with half of the movers going to Albuquerque and the other half to one of the
large cities. The Navaho and Zuni movers tend to
prefer a large city, whereas the Pueblo movers tend
to prefer Albuquerque. It should be pointed out
here that the Southern Pueblos are not very far
from Albuquerque, so even though it was carefully
specified that the Albuquerque alternative meant actually leaving the reservation as opposed to commuting, there would still be good opportunities for
frequent and close contacts with the reservations.
More females than males would prefer to leave their
present community (62 percent versus 53 percent),
and more of the respondents continuing their education beyond high school would prefer to leave than

TABLE 32

Relative Frequency of Location Preferences of New Mexico and
Arizona Indian High School Seniors for their Present
Community, Albuquerque, and Chicago, Los Angeles,
or the San Francisco Bay Area, under Differing
Wage Structure Assumptions

Case and Location Preference	Hourly Wage ($)	All Respondents (%)	Navahos (%)	Zunis (%)	Northern Pueblos (%)	Southern Pueblos (%)	Males (%)	Females (%)	Higher Education (%)	No Higher Education (%)
I Present community	1.50	43	44	46	49	31	47	38	42	49
Albuquerque	1.50	29	24	22	28	51	24	35	29	29
Chicago, Los Angeles, or San Francisco	1.50	28	32	32	23	18	29	27	29	22
II Present community	1.50	19	24	15	16	8	20	18	19	20
Albuquerque	1.75	38	29	42	40	61	35	41	39	35
Chicago, Los Angeles, or San Francisco	2.00	43	47	42	44	31	45	41	42	45

112

III Present community	1.50	17	23	9	13	7	16	17	16	21
Albuquerque	2.00	38	29	46	35	58	38	38	38	34
Chicago, Los Angeles, or San Francisco	2.50	45	48	45	52	35	46	45	46	44
IV Present community	1.50	16	22	10	9	7	16	16	15	21
Albuquerque	2.25	33	27	44	24	48	32	33	33	33
Chicago, Los Angeles, or San Francisco	3.00	51	51	46	67	45	52	51	52	46
V Present community	1.50	13	17	12	4	5	13	12	12	14
Albuquerque	2.50	35	31	36	33	50	30	40	35	36
Chicago, Los Angeles, or San Francisco	3.50	52	52	52	63	45	57	48	53	50
VI Present community	1.50	15	21	9	7	8	15	16	15	20
Albuquerque	3.50	32	28	29	31	49	29	36	31	40
Chicago, Los Angeles, or San Francisco	5.50	52	51	62	62	43	56	48	54	40
VII Present community	3.50	61	56	73	78	55	64	57	61	57
Albuquerque	2.50	25	25	20	12	37	21	29	25	27
Chicago, Los Angeles, or San Francisco	1.50	14	19	7	10	8	15	14	14	17
VIII Present community	1.50	16	22	8	6	7	15	17	15	21
Albuquerque	3.50	64	52	78	83	81	66	62	66	53
Chicago, Los Angeles, or San Francisco	2.50	20	26	14	11	12	19	21	19	26

would those finishing their education (58 percent
versus 51 percent). Male movers tend to prefer a
large city, but female movers show an even more pronounced tendency to prefer Albuquerque. Movers
among respondents who are not continuing their education tend to prefer Albuquerque; movers who are
continuing their education are equally divided between Albuquerque and a large city.

Cases II through VI and Case VIII indicate
that, when there is any economic advantage to moving, relatively few respondents would remain in
their present community. Even with the small wage
differentials shown in Case II, the proportion preferring to remain at home varies from 8 percent for
the Southern Pueblos to only 24 percent for the
Navahos. Even in Case VII, where the wage is con-
siderably higher at home than in the cities, 39
percent of the respondents would migrate (curiously,
where in the other cases the Navahos were the most
prone to remain in their present community, 44 percent would migrate even though they could make more
money at home).

A comparison of Cases V and VIII, which reverse
the wage rates in Albuquerque and the large city
while holding that in the home community constant,
indicates a clear tendency for each subgroup to prefer Albuquerque. It also should be noted that when
the wage is increased by $2.00 per hour in the large
city--between Cases V and VI--only the Zunis would
be more attracted to the large city.

In Table 33, Denver is substituted for Chicago-
Los Angeles-San Francisco Bay Area. The result is
to increase the proportion of movers and to increase
the proportion that would now favor the large-city
alternative. Nevertheless a comparison of Cases V
and VIII again indicates that a higher proportion
of the movers in each group prefers Albuquerque to
Denver.

The respondents were also asked "If you would
leave the place where you live now, would your decision where to go be influenced by where friends
and relatives have gone?" Forty-four percent of
all respondents replied in the affirmative. Of
this group, 18 percent stated the influence would

TABLE 33

Relative Frequency of Location Preferences of New Mexico
and Arizona Indian High School Seniors for their
Present Community, Albuquerque, and Denver,
under Differing Wage Structure Assumptions

Case and Location Preference	Hourly Wage ($)	All Respondents (%)	Navahos (%)	Zunis (%)	Northern Pueblos (%)	Southern Pueblos (%)	Males (%)	Females (%)	Higher Education (%)	No Higher Education (%)
I Present community	1.50	40	37	41	57	37	44	37	41	37
Albuquerque	1.50	24	18	37	23	35	21	26	23	29
Denver	1.50	36	45	22	20	28	35	37	36	34
II Present community	1.50	17	18	19	12	15	17	16	17	19
Albuquerque	1.75	29	23	39	45	33	29	30	30	23
Denver	2.00	54	59	42	43	52	54	54	53	58
III Present community	1.50	14	17	7	10	10	13	15	14	11
Albuquerque	2.00	27	21	35	34	39	28	27	28	20
Denver	2.50	59	62	58	56	51	59	58	58	69
IV Present community	1.50	13	17	10	9	7	11	16	14	10
Albuquerque	2.25	28	21	32	26	46	29	27	27	33
Denver	3.00	59	62	58	65	47	60	57	59	57
V Present community	1.50	13	16	10	4	10	12	13	13	11
Albuquerque	2.50	29	24	34	30	41	29	30	29	33
Denver	3.50	58	60	56	66	49	59	57	58	56
VI Present community	1.50	13	16	10	7	10	13	13	13	16
Albuquerque	3.50	27	23	34	20	40	25	29	26	31
Denver	5.50	60	61	56	73	50	62	58	61	53
VII Present community	3.50	58	53	64	78	56	61	55	59	48
Albuquerque	2.50	24	24	19	15	29	20	27	23	29
Denver	1.50	18	23	17	7	15	19	18	18	23
VIII Present community	1.50	17	23	12	6	10	16	19	18	16
Albuquerque	3.50	61	49	71	83	75	61	59	61	53
Denver	2.50	22	28	17	11	15	23	22	21	31

be weak, 54 percent said it would be moderate, and
28 percent said it would be strong. The Northern
Pueblo respondents were most likely to be influenced
by friends and relatives (54 percent, of which 86
percent indicated a moderate or strong influence)
whereas the Southern Pueblo respondents were the
least likely (36 percent, of which 74 percent indicated a moderate or strong influence).

Expected place of residence is shown in Table
34. The question posed in this regard was "Where
do you expect to be living five years from now, assuming your education and/or military service are
completed?" Seventy-four percent of all the respondents expected to be living off the reservations,
with the proportion ranging from 65 percent in the
case of the Northern Pueblos to 79 percent in the
case of the Zunis.

The regression equations in Table 35 show the
proportion of respondents preferring to remain in
their present community as a function of the opportunity cost (defined as before). None of the R^2
values is significant at the 5 percent level. The
reason is apparent. In Table 32, for example, 61
percent of all respondents would remain at home when
the wage is the highest there (Case VII), and 43
percent would remain when the wage is everywhere the
same (Case I). There is a further sharp decline to
19 percent once there is any economic advantage to
moving (Case II), but then the magnitude of the wage
differentials has no effect on the proportion of respondents who would move. In other words there is
a relatively small but stable number of respondents
who are attached to the reservation whatever the opportunity cost.

In summary, then, Indian reservations generally
have few relative advantages--other than cheap labor--
that would attract industry. It is not surprising,
therefore, that government programs to promote economic development have met with only very limited
success. On the other hand it is widely maintained
that Indians are particularly reluctant to leave
their native habitat in search of better opportunities elsewhere, and that when they do their destinations are likely to be big-city slums. In contrast

TABLE 34

Expected Place of Residence in Five Years of New Mexico
and Arizona Indian High School Seniors
(percentage)

Group	Present Community	Albuquerque	Chicago, Los Angeles, or San Francisco	Denver	Elsewhere
			Proportion Expecting to Live in		
All respondents	26	18	18	13	25
Navahos	23	16	17	17	27
Zunis	21	19	15	9	36
Northern Pueblos	35	19	22	7	17
Southern Pueblos	33	22	22	8	15
Males	29	15	19	13	24
Females	24	20	18	14	24
Higher education	26	17	18	13	26
No higher education	25	25	21	16	13

117

TABLE 35

Regressions Relating Opportunity Cost (X) to Percentage of Respondents
Preferring to Remain in their Present Community (Y)

Group	With Chicago, Los Angeles, San Francisco Bay Alternative		With Denver Alternative	
	Regression Equation	R^2	Regression Equation	R^2
All respondents	Y=-11.70+.268X	.60	Y=-11.36+.275X	.58
Navahos	Y=-14.74+.340X	.60	Y=-13.20+.333X	.55
Zunis	Y= -9.39+.193X	.58	Y= -9.93+.228X	.59
Northern Pueblos	Y= -9.10+.180X	.63	Y= -8.76+.164X	.59
Southern Pueblos	Y= -8.93+.246X	.53	Y=-10.05+.261X	.58
Males	Y=-11.33+.246X	.60	Y=-10.71+.244X	.57
Females	Y=-11.99+.293X	.57	Y=-12.02+.305X	.58
Continuing higher education	Y=-11.42+.263X	.59	Y=-11.38+.270X	.58
Not continuing higher education	Y=-12.84+.281X	.54	Y=-11.45+.307X	.50

the present study indicates that Indian high school
seniors, who represent the future leadership of the
reservations, if not the future survival of the
tribes in geographically localized places, are for
the most part quite willing to leave for better opportunities elsewhere. This is particularly striking in view of the fact that the tribes concerned
are considered to be among the more successful in
the nation in achieving a stable reconciliation of
traditional values with those of the larger society.

If Indian populations are to be given greater
opportunity to participate equally in national economic progress there must be vastly greater investment in human resources on the reservations, including programs that, while respecting Indian culture,
bring sociological behavior more into line with the
kind of outlook needed for stable employment. While
this may further increase outmigration, sentiment
about reservation life--which is encountered more
among older Indian leaders and well-meaning whites
than among young Indians--should not obscure the
fact that the matching of workers and jobs demands
a broader geographic perspective than is available
by concentrating on the reservations themselves.

It may finally be noted that the Indians were
not asked to state their preferences with and without the availability of relocation assistance.
This was because the Employment Assistance Program
of the Bureau of Indian Affairs provides for fairly
comprehensive voluntary relocation assistance. Of
the respondents who expected to migrate, 65 percent
stated that they intended to use the services of
the Employment Assistance Program. Moreover only
32 percent of those who expected to migrate without
BIA assistance felt that the program was unsatisfactory. Thus the principal difficulty with the assistance program in the light of the present study is
that it is perhaps too oriented toward large cities
and not enough toward job opportunities in intermediate centers.

SOUTHWEST MISSISSIPPI

The results of the Mississippi survey are similar to those in the other regions, except that
blacks show a stronger preference for large distant
cities than for intermediate centers. The data in
Table 36 indicate that, with wage rates the same in
each alternative (Case I), nearly 70 percent of all
respondents would stay at home, with the subgroup
proportion ranging from 65 percent for blacks to 76
percent for males. But once there is even a small
advantage to moving, as in Case II, the proportion
who would stay at home declines to about 40 percent,
with blacks and females being the most prone to
leave and whites and males the least. As the financial advantage to moving becomes greater, there is
a pronounced tendency for the proportion who would
move to increase. Case IV provides a useful example
of some of the general tendencies. In this case
only 16.6 percent of all the respondents would stay
home. However, even though the big-city wage is
$3.00 and that in the intermediate city only $2.25,
more people prefer the intermediate city. Females
prefer the intermediate city more than males do,
and the respondents not going to college favor it
over those going to college. But the most important factor is race: whites who would prefer to
move prefer the intermediate city by a ratio of well
over two to one. Blacks, on the other hand, prefer
the big city outside of the South by about the same
margin.

In Case VI, where the intermediate-city wage
is the highest of the three alternatives, 87.7 percent of the whites prefer the intermediate city.
And 74.4 percent of the blacks also prefer it. But
when the wage rates in the intermediate and big
city are reversed, with that in the home community
held constant (Case VII), whites still prefer the
intermediate city by 56 percent to 30 percent.
Blacks, in contrast, again choose the high wage in
the big city, the ratio being 59 percent to 27 percent.

The data in Table 37 show the relative frequency of location preferences, assuming the

TABLE 36

Relative Frequency of Location Preferences of Southwest Mississippi Young People for their Present Community, for Jackson, Memphis, or Baton Rouge, and for Chicago, Detroit, Los Angeles, or Houston, by Selected Groups

Case and Location Preference	Hourly Wage ($)	All (%)	Males (%)	Females (%)	Whites (%)	Blacks (%)	College-Bound (%)	Noncollege-Bound (%)
I Present community	1.50	69.4	75.7	63.1	73.9	64.6	69.1	69.3
Jackson, Memphis, Baton Rouge	1.50	18.2	13.6	23.5	20.9	15.3	17.1	19.5
Chicago, Detroit, Los Angeles, Houston		12.4	10.7	13.4	5.2	20.1	13.7	11.2
II Present community	1.50	39.2	44.0	33.5	44.9	33.0	35.4	43.1
Jackson, Memphis, Baton Rouge	1.75	31.1	27.8	36.2	39.6	22.0	30.2	31.4
Chicago, Detroit, Los Angeles, Houston	2.00	29.7	28.2	30.3	15.4	45.0	34.4	25.5
III Present community	1.50	24.4	27.4	21.3	28.1	20.4	19.9	29.1
Jackson, Memphis, Baton Rouge	2.00	42.7	40.1	46.2	54.1	30.5	40.9	43.8
Chicago, Detroit, Los Angeles, Houston	2.50	32.9	32.4	32.5	17.8	49.1	39.3	27.1
IV Present community	1.50	16.6	17.7	16.0	17.8	15.5	11.9	21.6
Jackson, Memphis, Baton Rouge	2.25	42.2	46.5	44.7	56.5	27.0	39.2	44.7
Chicago, Detroit, Los Angeles, Houston	3.00	41.1	41.8	39.3	25.7	57.6	48.9	33.7
V Present community	3.50	82.3	85.1	79.3	82.8	81.7	81.6	82.8
Jackson, Memphis, Baton Rouge	2.50	11.3	8.6	14.2	13.7	8.7	11.6	11.2
Chicago, Detroit, Los Angeles, Houston		6.4	6.2	6.5	3.4	9.6	6.9	6.1
VI Present community	1.50	9.4	9.8	8.9	7.4	11.5	7.4	11.0
Jackson, Memphis, Baton Rouge	3.50	81.3	81.3	87.3	87.7	74.4	82.7	80.1
Chicago, Detroit, Los Angeles, Houston	2.50	9.4	8.9	9.8	4.9	14.1	9.8	8.9
VII Present community	1.50	13.7	14.6	13.1	13.5	13.9	10.0	17.5
Jackson, Memphis, Baton Rouge	2.50	41.9	39.3	44.4	56.0	26.8	37.9	45.4
Chicago, Detroit, Los Angeles, Houston	3.50	44.4	46.1	42.5	30.0	59.4	52.1	37.1
VIII Present community	1.50	7.7	8.0	7.3	7.7	7.8	4.4	11.0
Jackson, Memphis, Baton Rouge	3.50	31.9	30.2	34.2	44.7	18.3	26.9	36.6
Chicago, Detroit, Los Angeles, Houston	5.50	60.4	61.8	58.5	47.7	73.9	68.7	52.4

TABLE 37

Relative Frequency of Location Preferences of Southwest Mississippi Young People, if there were a Government Relocation Assistance Program, by Selected Groups

Case and Location Preference	Hourly Wage ($)	All (%)	Males (%)	Females (%)	Whites (%)	Blacks (%)	College-Bound (%)	Noncollege-Bound (%)
I Present community	1.50	63.8	72.7	53.8	66.3	61.1	60.8	66.3
Jackson, Memphis, Baton Rouge	1.50	21.7	15.8	28.5	25.8	17.3	22.1	21.8
Chicago, Detroit, Los Angeles, Houston		14.5	11.6	17.7	8.0	21.6	17.1	11.9
II Present community	1.50	37.6	45.0	28.5	43.9	31.1	32.9	42.5
Jackson, Memphis, Baton Rouge	1.75	31.0	27.2	36.4	38.7	22.9	31.3	31.1
Chicago, Detroit, Los Angeles, Houston		31.3	27.8	35.1	17.5	46.0	35.8	26.4
III Present community	1.50	25.9	30.6	20.7	29.0	22.6	21.3	30.4
Jackson, Memphis, Baton Rouge	2.00	42.4	40.0	45.1	50.9	33.5	40.9	44.0
Chicago, Detroit, Los Angeles, Houston		31.7	29.4	34.1	20.1	44.0	37.9	25.5
IV Present community	1.50	15.2	17.4	12.3	17.2	13.1	10.4	20.2
Jackson, Memphis, Baton Rouge	2.25	41.5	46.3	43.5	52.9	29.3	38.1	44.9
Chicago, Detroit, Los Angeles, Houston	3.00	43.3	42.3	44.2	29.8	57.6	51.4	34.9
V Present community	3.50	81.4	86.6	76.5	82.8	79.9	80.5	82.3
Jackson, Memphis, Baton Rouge	2.50	12.5	8.2	16.6	13.8	11.0	13.1	12.0
Chicago, Detroit, Los Angeles, Houston	1.50	6.1	5.1	6.9	3.4	9.0	6.4	5.8
VI Present community	1.50	8.7	9.9	7.2	6.6	11.1	6.3	11.1
Jackson, Memphis, Baton Rouge	3.50	82.0	82.2	81.8	88.7	74.8	83.8	80.4
Chicago, Detroit, Los Angeles, Houston	2.50	9.3	8.0	11.0	4.8	14.1	10.0	8.5
VII Present community	1.50	11.7	12.9	10.1	12.3	11.1	7.7	15.8
Jackson, Memphis, Baton Rouge	2.50	41.9	40.5	42.5	53.7	28.5	38.6	44.4
Chicago, Detroit, Los Angeles, Houston	3.50	46.8	46.6	47.3	34.0	60.4	53.6	39.9
III Present community	1.50	6.2	6.8	5.3	6.6	5.7	3.3	9.1
Jackson, Memphis, Baton Rouge	3.50	31.6	30.8	32.5	41.7	20.9	25.9	37.2
Chicago, Detroit, Los Angeles, Houston	5.50	62.2	62.4	62.1	51.7	73.4	70.8	53.6

availability of government relocation assistance.
When all respondents are considered, there is a
drop in the proportion who would stay at home in
Case I from 69.4 to 63.8 percent. In the other
cases, however, relocation assistance does not make
much difference in the response patterns. For each
of the subgroups, relocation assistance is most influential when wage differences among different
places are nonexistent or small. When there is no
difference (Case I), females are particularly responsive to relocation assistance. The proportion
who would stay at home drops from 63.1 percent without assistance to 53.8 percent with assistance. In
Case II there is a corresponding drop of five percentage points. It is noteworthy that whites seem
more responsive to relocation assistance than blacks,
and that college-bound respondents seem more responsive than noncollege-bound respondents. In other
words the groups that are most likely to be relatively disadvantaged from an economic viewpoint are
less likely to take advantage of relocation assistance. It is not apparent to the author why this
pattern obtains, but it suggests a need for considerable outreach efforts in relocation assistance
programs aimed at relatively disadvantaged persons.

     The respondents were asked about the degree to
which their choice of residence would be influenced
by where they had friends and relatives. Thirty-
four percent stated that they would be "very much"
or "completely" influenced by friends and relatives.
No group varied by more than three percentage points
from this figure.

     Expected place of residence after school and
military obligations are fulfilled are shown in
Table 38. Only 29 percent of all the respondents
expect to remain in their present community. In
the case of males, whites, and noncollege-bound respondents, between 36 and 38 percent of each group
expects to remain at home; in the case of females,
blacks, and noncollege-bound respondents, the corresponding figures are only 20 to 22 percent. It is
striking that 71 percent of the whites expect to
either remain at home or live in one of the specified intermediate-sized cities, whereas this is the

TABLE 38

Expected Place of Residence in Five Years of Southwest
Mississippi Respondents, by Selected Groups

		Proportion Expecting to Live in		
Group	Present Community	Jackson, Memphis, Baton Rouge	Chicago, Detroit, Los Angeles, Houston	Elsewhere
All respondents	29	24	25	22
Males	37	21	23	20
Females	20	30	26	25
Whites	38	33	5	25
Blacks	20	15	46	20
College-bound	22	23	30	25
Noncollege-bound	36	25	19	20

case for only 35 percent of the blacks, about half
of whom expect to live in one of the specified big
cities.

The regression equations in Table 39 show the
proportion of respondents preferring to remain in
their present community as a function of the opportunity cost (as defined in the other case studies).
Even without relocation assistance, the R^2 values
are high, ranging from .744 in the case of the
Academy students to .831 in the case of the MDTA
trainees. The R^2 values with relocation assistance
are higher for every group; they range from .823 in
the case of black respondents to .908 for the Academy
students. The rather dramatic reversal of positions
for the Academy respondents may be partly accounted
for by the small sample size of this group. In any
case the overall evidence suggests that the availability of relocation assistance would increase responsiveness to the opportunity cost of remaining
at home.

EASTERN KENTUCKY--1971

The last of the studies was again made among
high school seniors in the Big Sandy region of eastern Kentucky. In comparing the results shown in
Table 40 with those presented in Table 23, it is
evident that the preference patterns have remained
fairly stable. For all respondents there is an increase in Case I of 5.2 percentage points in the
relative frequency of those who would remain in
eastern Kentucky, but the shift is almost wholly at
the expense of northern cities rather than of intermediate cities. Cases II, III, V, and VI are very
similar, whereas Cases IV, VII, and VIII again evidence some shift from northern cities to eastern
Kentucky. The proportion favoring the intermediate
cities is especially stable, although in Case VI,
where the intermediate-city wage is highest, there
is an increase of 4.6 percentage points between the
studies. Females are still much more inclined to
leave eastern Kentucky than are males, and females
show a relatively stronger preference for the intermediate cities than was the case two years earlier.

TABLE 39

Regressions Relating Opportunity Cost (X) to Percentage of Students
Preferring to Remain in Southwest Mississippi (Y)

Group	Without Relocation Assistance			With Relocation Assistance		
	Regression Equation	R^2	t	Regression Equation	R^2	t
All students	Y=4.91+3.64X	.807	5.01	Y=4.77+3.63X	.839	5.59
Males	Y=5.27+3.86X	.802	4.92	Y=5.32+3.96X	.832	5.44
Females	Y=4.58+3.46X	.814	5.13	Y=4.20+3.37X	.834	5.48
Whites	Y=5.17+3.81X	.800	4.90	Y=5.00+3.76X	.838	5.57
Blacks	Y=4.70+3.51X	.801	4.90	Y=4.52+3.50X	.823	5.29
Academy	Y=5.67+4.58X	.744	4.18	Y=5.59+4.76X	.908	5.31
Public high school	Y=4.57+3.63X	.800	4.89	Y=4.34+3.54X	.827	5.35
MDTA	Y=5.90+3.28X	.831	5.43	Y=5.92+3.46X	.864	6.16
Junior college	Y=5.25+3.72X	.816	5.16	Y=5.19+3.77X	.834	5.49

TABLE 40

Relative Frequency of Location Preferences of Eastern Kentucky
High School Seniors, By Selected Groups, 1971

Case and Location Preference	Hourly Wage ($)	All Respondents (%)	Males (%)	Females (%)	Lived Outside (%)	Never Outside (%)	4-year College (%)	Junior College (%)	Vocational (%)	No More School (%)
I Eastern Kentucky	1.50	69.4	72.7	66.9	64.0	71.3	57.9	68.1	70.8	78.7
Lexington, Louisville	1.50	24.0	18.2	28.4	25.2	23.6	33.1	26.4	20.8	17.0
Northern City	1.50	6.6	9.4	4.7	10.8	5.1	9.0	5.6	8.3	4.3
II Eastern Kentucky	1.50	24.3	29.3	20.3	25.7	23.3	17.6	28.2	47.6	25.1
Lexington, Louisville	1.75	38.3	33.0	42.4	30.9	41.1	47.7	42.3	19.0	32.5
Northern City	2.00	37.4	37.7	37.2	43.4	35.6	34.7	29.6	33.3	42.5
III Eastern Kentucky	1.50	16.3	19.2	13.9	17.8	15.4	12.7	19.4	36.4	14.9
Lexington, Louisville	2.00	39.8	31.8	45.8	32.6	42.1	45.1	41.7	31.8	36.4
Northern City	2.50	43.9	49.1	40.3	49.6	42.4	42.2	38.9	31.8	48.7
IV Eastern Kentucky	1.50	13.5	14.2	12.7	12.9	13.6	9.6	16.7	38.1	12.4
Lexington, Louisville	2.25	36.9	32.0	40.8	34.3	37.6	43.8	43.1	33.3	30.3
Northern City	3.00	49.6	53.9	46.6	52.9	48.8	46.6	40.3	28.6	57.3
V Eastern Kentucky	3.50	83.5	86.9	80.8	81.0	84.4	76.4	85.9	90.9	87.7
Lexington, Louisville	2.50	13.8	10.8	16.2	13.9	13.7	21.3	12.7	9.1	9.3
Northern City	1.50	2.7	2.3	3.1	5.1	1.9	2.2	1.4	0.0	3.0
VI Eastern Kentucky	1.50	9.9	9.2	10.2	10.6	9.6	4.0	8.2	38.1	12.3
Lexington, Louisville	3.50	85.7	86.2	85.6	81.8	87.2	90.4	91.8	57.1	82.8
Northern City	2.50	4.4	4.6	4.2	7.6	3.3	5.6	0.0	4.8	4.8
VII Eastern Kentucky	1.50	12.5	11.0	13.3	12.5	12.1	8.5	8.5	35.0	13.9
Lexington, Louisville	2.50	35.9	32.6	38.6	29.4	38.0	44.3	43.7	35.0	27.8
Northern City	3.50	51.6	56.4	48.1	58.1	49.9	47.2	47.9	30.0	58.3
VIII Eastern Kentucky	1.50	8.9	6.3	10.7	8.7	8.8	4.5	6.9	35.0	10.4
Lexington, Louisville	3.50	27.3	21.0	32.3	17.4	30.6	36.9	27.8	20.0	20.8
Northern City	5.50	63.8	72.8	57.0	73.9	60.6	58.5	65.3	45.0	68.8

The question of whether the respondents had
ever lived outside of eastern Kentucky was not
raised in the 1969 survey. With the exception of
Case I, where those who had lived outside are less
attached to eastern Kentucky, there is not much difference on this issue. However there are some
notable differences among the groups on the place
to which they would prefer to move. In these cases
there is a clear tendency for those who have never
resided outside the region to prefer Lexington or
Louisville to the northern city alternative.

In the 1969 survey the students were broken
down on the basis of those who were going on to college and those who were not. However, because the
alternatives are not always that simple, the 1971
survey distinguished among four categories: those
going on to a four-year college, to a junior college, to a vocational school, or to no school. The
vocational training group showed a much stronger
preference for eastern Kentucky than did any of the
other groups, perhaps because they are preparing
for jobs in the region; on the other hand the small
sample size may have resulted in a relatively large
sampling variation. In any event it may be said
with confidence that the least likely people to remain in the region are those going on to four-year
colleges. These persons also have a relatively
strong preference for Lexington and Louisville.
There is a less pronounced relative preference for
northern cities on the part of those not continuing
their education or training. Because this group is
the one most immediately confronted with the need
to make a choice concerning place of residence and
employment, it is perhaps the most likely to follow
traditional migration paths to the North.

Table 41 shows the relative frequency of responses assuming the existence of a government relocation assistance program. Preferences as such
do not seem to be greatly affected by this assumption. In Cases I and V the proportion of all respondents who would remain in eastern Kentucky is
reduced by 3.6 percentage points, but in no other
case is the difference even this great. Availability of relocation assistance affects the preferences

TABLE 41

Relative Frequency of Location Preferences of Eastern Kentucky High School Seniors,
if there were a Government Relocation Assistance Program,
by Selected Groups, 1971

Case and Location Preference	Hourly Wage ($)	All Respondents (%)	Males (%)	Females (%)	Lived Outside (%)	Never Outside (%)	4-year College (%)	Junior College (%)	Vocational (%)	No More School (%)
I Eastern Kentucky	1.50	65.9	75.2	58.7	61.3	67.5	53.4	61.1	78.3	75.4
Lexington, Louisville	1.50	25.0	17.4	30.8	25.5	24.8	36.2	33.3	21.7	14.5
Northern City	1.50	9.1	7.3	10.5	13.1	7.7	10.3	5.6	0.0	10.1
II Eastern Kentucky	1.50	24.5	32.1	18.5	20.4	25.8	18.4	28.2	47.6	26.2
Lexington, Louisville	1.75	35.5	29.8	39.9	33.6	35.8	48.3	39.4	38.1	24.5
Northern City	2.00	40.0	38.1	41.6	46.0	38.3	33.3	32.4	14.3	49.3
III Eastern Kentucky	1.50	15.2	19.0	12.1	14.1	15.6	13.3	19.7	33.3	13.7
Lexington, Louisville	2.00	40.3	36.6	43.3	36.3	41.5	49.1	43.7	42.9	32.6
Northern City	2.50	44.5	44.4	44.7	49.6	42.9	37.6	36.6	23.8	53.7
IV Eastern Kentucky	1.50	11.2	9.9	11.8	10.5	11.3	8.3	12.5	28.6	11.1
Lexington, Louisville	2.25	38.7	35.2	41.6	34.6	40.0	49.7	47.2	28.6	29.2
Northern City	3.00	50.1	54.9	46.6	54.9	48.7	42.0	40.3	42.9	59.7
V Eastern Kentucky	3.50	79.9	82.7	77.8	78.5	80.7	74.4	83.6	85.7	82.2
Lexington, Louisville	2.50	14.6	12.6	16.0	14.1	14.4	19.3	15.1	9.5	11.3
Northern City	1.50	5.5	4.7	6.1	7.4	4.9	6.3	1.4	4.8	6.5
VI Eastern Kentucky	1.50	9.2	7.9	9.8	8.1	9.4	5.2	8.3	33.3	9.1
Lexington, Louisville	3.50	85.5	87.0	84.6	83.1	86.4	88.4	88.9	57.1	85.7
Northern City	2.50	5.4	5.1	5.6	8.8	4.2	6.4	2.8	9.5	5.2
VII Eastern Kentucky	1.50	11.0	9.9	11.5	9.6	11.4	7.6	9.9	33.3	10.9
Lexington, Louisville	2.50	39.2	37.7	40.4	38.2	39.0	47.7	43.7	33.3	32.8
Northern City	3.50	49.8	52.4	48.1	52.2	49.6	44.8	46.5	33.3	56.3
VIII Eastern Kentucky	1.50	7.6	5.9	8.7	7.3	7.6	4.7	6.9	23.8	8.4
Lexington, Louisville	3.50	30.3	25.2	34.4	23.4	32.5	36.0	33.3	28.6	25.2
Northern City	5.50	62.0	68.9	56.9	69.3	59.9	59.3	59.7	47.6	66.4

of females slightly more than those of males, people
who have lived elsewhere more than those who have
not, and people in vocational training more than the
other education subgroups. The data in Table 42 indicate that the comparable groups are more responsive
to opportunity cost in the 1971 survey than in the
1969 survey, and that availability of relocation assistance increases the responsiveness even more for
all groups.

The greatest difference in the two surveys is
reflected in the data in Table 43, which indicate
that there is a substantial increase in the proportion of respondents who expect to live in eastern
Kentucky in five years. The better educated and
those who have lived outside the region before have
a higher expectation of living elsewhere. Among
those expecting to live outside of eastern Kentucky,
the four-year college and junior college groups have
a relatively high proportion of persons expecting to
live in Lexington or Louisville. In view of the
relative stability of location preferences, it is
difficult to explain the increase in the expectations of living in eastern Kentucky. It is possible
that the prospect of better opportunities in the region may make more of those who prefer eastern Kentucky actually expect to live there. Another factor may be the substantial increase in unemployment
nationally between 1969 and 1971. The most dramatic
increases in expectations of living in eastern Kentucky were among the vocational and no-more-school
groups, as well as among those who had never lived
outside of the region; these people may feel that,
in view of their educational attainment and lack of
experience in the "outside" world, it is reasonable
to expect to remain at home, at least assuming the
continuation of generally high unemployment across
the nation.

SUMMARY

For ease of comparison, the location preferences
of all respondents in each area surveyed are summarized in Table 44. In the data shown here, the large-
city options for the Indians were Chicago, Los Angeles,

Regressions Relating Opportunity Cost (X) to Percentage of Students
Preferring to Remain in Eastern Kentucky (Y), 1971

Group	Without Relocation Assistance			With Relocation Assistance		
	Regression Equation	R^2	t	Regression Equation	R^2	t
All students	Y=4.55+3.54X	.719	3.91	Y=4.37+3.47X	.729	4.01
Males	Y=4.86+3.91X	.765	4.41	Y=4.77+3.85X	.744	4.82
Females	Y=4.36+3.34X	.678	3.55	Y=4.07+3.20X	.706	3.79
Four-year college	Y=3.90+3.35X	.734	4.07	Y=3.74+3.21X	.749	4.23
Junior college	Y=4.72+3.78X	.775	4.54	Y=4.52+3.63X	.794	4.81
Vocational	Y=6.05+2.57X	.742	4.15	Y=5.88+2.95X	.767	4.44
No more school	Y=4.90+3.80X	.679	3.56	Y=4.60+3.67X	.694	3.68

TABLE 43

Expected Place of Residence in Five Years of Eastern Kentucky
Seniors, by Selected Groups, 1971

Group	Eastern Kentucky	Proportion Expecting to Live in		
		Lexington, Louisville	Northern City	Elsewhere
All respondents	55.1	15.8	16.8	12.3
Males	58.8	14.4	15.0	11.8
Females	52.4	16.7	18.1	12.8
Live outside	44.8	15.2	22.9	17.1
Never outside	59.2	16.2	14.0	10.7
Four-year college	40.7	29.7	7.6	22.0
Junior college	50.0	28.3	13.0	8.7
Vocational	68.4	0.0	21.1	10.5
No more school	63.4	6.3	23.0	7.3

TABLE 44

Relative Frequency of Preferences for Home Areas, Intermediate Centers, and Large Cities, by Selected Groups of Young Persons

Case and Location Preference	Hourly Wage ($)	Eastern Kentucky (1969) (%)	Eastern Kentucky (1971) (%)	Mexican Americans in South Texas (%)	South-western Indians (%)	Southwest Mississippi	
						Blacks (%)	Whites (%)
I Home area	1.50	64	69	75	43	65	74
Intermediate center	1.50	26	24	15	29	15	21
Large city	1.50	10	7	10	28	20	5
II Home area	1.50	25	24	42	19	33	45
Intermediate center	1.75	36	38	23	38	22	40
Large city	2.00	39	37	35	43	45	15
III Home area	1.50	18	16	31	17	20	28
Intermediate center	2.00	40	40	34	38	30	54
Large city	2.50	42	44	35	45	49	18
IV Home area	1.50	10	14	21	16	16	18
Intermediate center	2.25	36	37	38	33	27	56
Large city	3.00	54	50	41	51	58	26
V Home area	3.50	81	84	84	61	82	83
Intermediate center	2.50	13	14	11	25	9	14
Large city	1.50	5	3	5	14	10	3
VI Home area	1.50	10	10	20	16	12	7
Intermediate center	3.50	81	86	76	64	74	88
Large city	2.50	9	4	4	20	14	5
VII Home area	1.50	9	12	20	13	14	14
Intermediate center	2.50	35	36	37	35	27	56
Large city	3.50	56	52	43	52	59	30
VIII Home area	1.50	6	9	14	15	8	8
Intermediate center	3.50	27	27	30	32	18	45
Large city	5.50	66	64	56	52	74	48

and the San Francisco Bay Area. For the other groups
they were Chicago and Detroit. The intermediate
cities for eastern Kentucky were Lexington and Louisville; for the Mexican Americans, San Antonio and
Corpus Christi; for the Indians, Albuquerque; and
for the Mississippians, Baton Rouge, Jackson, and
Memphis.

It is evident that mobility potential is quite
high. Many persons would move even though there
were no economic advantage (Case I). Once there is
any economic advantage at all to moving (Case II),
the proportion who would prefer to leave their present area varies from 55 percent in the case of Mississippi whites to 81 percent in the case of the
Indians. In general the preference patterns are
clearly influenced by the structure of relative
wages. With the exception of Mississippi blacks,
there is also a pronounced tendency for movers to
prefer intermediate centers to large cities. This
is perhaps best seen by comparing Case VI with Case
VII, which reverse the wages in the intermediate
and large cities, while that in the home community
holds constant.

While these findings do not necessarily apply
either to persons who dropped out of high school or
to older persons, they are consistent with the position that relatively more attention should be given
in public policy to linking people in lagging areas
to opportunities in intermediate centers. "For example," Huber and Ullman argue, "students in rural
high schools could make much better decisions concerning migration, and would waste less time search-
ing randomly, if they had access to current job
bank books from nearby cities. The possible use of
job bank data to influence migration flows is an
intriguing area for study."[2] Moreover the need for
this and related forms of assistance is made even
more compelling by evidence that actual migration
of high school students is greater than intended
migration.[3]

5

MIGRATION CENTERS, GROWTH CENTERS, AND THE REGIONAL COMMISSIONS: AN ANALYSIS OF EXPECTED FUTURE LIFETIME INCOME GAINS TO MIGRANTS FROM LAGGING REGIONS

INTRODUCTION

In contrast to the preceding two chapters, which deal with the location preferences of persons in lagging and, for the most part, rural areas, this chapter analyzes actual migration from lagging areas to Standard Metropolitan Statistical Areas (SMSAs). However the coverage in this chapter is greater in terms of both areas and people. (Estimated migration from the four survey areas to SMSAs is presented in Appendix C.)

The analyses in this chapter are carried out within the context of the effort that has been made during the past decade by the federal government to promote the development of economically lagging areas of the nation. The Area Redevelopment Act of 1961 and the Accelerated Public Works Act of 1962 provided for investments in declining communities. Unfortunately insufficient funds, inadequate planning, and lack of attention to human resource development limited the impact of these acts.[1]

In 1965 the Appalachian Regional Development Act and the Public Works and Economic Development Act were passed to deal more efficiently and comprehensively with the problems of regions characterized by high unemployment and low income. The former created the Appalachian Regional Commission. The latter created the Economic Development Administration and provided for regional commissions

corresponding to the one set up for Appalachia. To
date such bodies, usually termed Title V commissions, have been established for the Ozarks, the
Four Corners, the Atlantic coastal plains, the upper Great Lakes, and New England. Except for the
New England one, all of the commissions deal with
areas that have been defined primarily in terms of
economic distress; i.e., regional boundaries delin-
eate lagging areas within which growth is to be en-
couraged by the commissions. The New England Regional Commission also is exceptional because it
includes whole states, whereas all of the others
include only parts of states. For these reasons it
is not included here.

Both of the 1965 acts stipulated that, in determining investment priorities, consideration
should be given to "the relationship of the project
or class of projects to overall regional development including its location in an area determined
by the State to have a significant potential for
growth."[2] Both acts also specified that consideration be given to the prospects that a project would
permanently "improve the opportunities for employment, the average level of income, or the economic
and social development of the area served by the
project." In keeping with their legislative mandate, the regional commissions have been oriented
toward "the area served by the project" (although
the Appalachian Regional Commission states that its
overall objectives include not only developing Appalachia but also providing every person in the region with the health and skills needed to compete
for opportunities anywhere he may choose to live[3]).

In this chapter, however, the implicit con-
straint that place welfare is to be maximized is
relaxed in favor of the assumption that places
should benefit people. Before raising a number of
policy issues within this context, it is necessary
to define the terms "migration center" and "growth
center."

Migration centers are SMSAs that are doing
most in relation to their own size to increase
lifetime incomes of migrants from lagging areas.
More specifically, data from a 1 percent Social

Security sample are used to analyze the income
gains of migrants from each regional commission
area (except New England) to each SMSA in the country. Migration centers are the highest ranking
SMSAs with respect to an index that consists of the
total increase in expected future lifetime income
of relevant migrants divided by the population of
the SMSA. The rationale for this index will be
discussed in some detail.

Growth centers are SMSAs in which population
growth from 1960 to 1970 was more rapid than in
SMSAs as a whole, which grew by 15.1 percent.

The purpose of this study is not simply to
identify migration centers benefiting people from
lagging areas but also to analyze their relationship to growth centers. It is our contention that
the regional legislation in question is correct in
calling for a growth-center strategy to benefit
disadvantaged people, but that its narrow geographic
focus precludes the selection of the most relevant
growth centers. So this study examines the extent
to which migration centers are in fact growth centers, and, if so, whether they are within regional
commission areas, within other parts of the migrants' home states, or in other states.

These issues have obvious policy implications
because, of the 24 states considered here, only one
(West Virginia) is entirely within a regional commission area. The rest are only partly covered by
commissions (the Carolinas and Georgia are partly
but not exhaustively covered by two commissions).
In particular, if the most relevant migration centers are growth centers within regional commission
states but outside of regional commission counties,
it would seem appropriate to include whole states
in planning for the creation of better economic opportunities for the people of the lagging areas.
The results in fact lend support to this position.

THE MIGRATION DATA

The migration data presented in this study were
obtained from 1 percent Social Security sample.

Their nature is discussed in Appendix C. For our purposes a migrant is defined as any person working in a regional commission area county in 1960 who worked in a different county in 1965. The 1965 counties include all SMSA counties in the United States. Persons who merely changed counties of employment within SMSAs have been excluded.*

(Although 1965 data were the latest available when this study was prepared, the results of the 1970 Census indicate that the migration trends of the 1960s were part of a fairly stable pattern extending back through the previous decade. This came as something of a surprise to those who expected a decline in migration from rural areas on the basis of erroneous 1966 estimates made by the Bureau of the Census.)

Migrants' Expected Future Lifetime Income
Increase in Relation to Size of
SMSA (M_{AB}): The Computation
Process

The present value of a migrant's expected future lifetime income, Y_e, is calculated in the following manner:

----

*Our work with the 1-percent sample over the past three years has indicated that non-SMSA counties draw few migrants from the regional commission areas. This is in keeping with a recent International Economic Association conference that concluded that "the general sense of our discussions was that the minimum size of growth points that experience had shown to be successful was nearer to a population of 100,000 than to one of 10,000, and that even 100,000 was more likely to be an underestimate than an overestimate." See E. A. G. Robinson, "Introduction," in Robinson, ed., Backward Areas in Advanced Countries (New York: St. Martin's Press, 1969), p. xvi.

$$Y_e = \left[\frac{\alpha_a}{\alpha_a} \left(\frac{1}{2} \right) \left(N_a \right) \; Y_m \right] \left[\frac{(1 + .034)^{\iota_a} - 1}{(1 + .060)^{\iota_a} - 1} \right]$$

$$+ \sum_{i = a+1}^{7} \left[\frac{\alpha_i}{\alpha_a} \left(N_i \right) \; Y_m \right] \left[\frac{(1 + .034)^{\iota_i} - 1}{(1 + .060)^{\iota_i} - 1} \right]$$

where α_i is the age-income index, N_i is the number of years in age class i, Y_m is the migrant's income in 1965, and ι_i is the number of years from 1965 to the last year in age class i. The age-income index values are shown by sex in Table 45.

TABLE 45

Age-Income Indexes (α_i), by Sex

Age Class (i)	Male	Female
(1)		
14–19	0.15	0.21
(2)		
20–24	1.00	1.00
(3)		
25–34	1.89	1.00
(4)		
35–44	2.13	1.22
(5)		
45–54	2.00	1.30
(6)		
55–64	1.67	0.98
(7)		
65–75	0.66	0.51

Note: The index values are based on the average of the median incomes for each age class for years 1958 through 1962.

Source: U.S. Bureau of the Census, "Consumer Income," Current Population Reports, Series P-60, Nos. 35, 37, 39, 41, 43, 47, 51, 53, 60, 75.

To calculate Y_e it is first necessary to multiply 1965 income by appropriate quotients of coefficients from Table 45. In the migrant's own age class, a, where

$$\frac{^a a}{^a a} = 1,$$

it is assumed that his age is at the class midpoint. Therefore only 1/2 N_a years remain in that class, whereas in the remaining classes we sum over all N_i years. For example a male migrant in the 25-34 age group (a = his group) is assumed to be at the midpoint of group i = 3. He will earn an unadjusted 1965 income Y_m for one-half of the remaining years that he will be in that class; i.e., 1/2 N_3 = 1/2(10) = 5. In the next decade of his life he will earn

$$\frac{^a 4}{^a 3} = \frac{2.13}{1.89} \; Y_m$$

for all N_4 = 10 years. Similarly he will earn

$$\frac{^a 5}{^a 3} = \frac{2.00}{1.89} \; Y_m$$

for each N_5 = 10 years when he is in the 45-54 age group. And so forth until he is in the final age group.

However future income needs to be adjusted for productivity gains and the whole future income stream needs to be discounted to its present value. Thus

$$\frac{(1 + .034)^{\iota} a^{-1}}{(1 + .060)^{\iota} a^{-1}}$$

represents an annual productivity and wage increase of 3.4 percent and a 6 percent rate of discount.[4]

If the given migrant had not moved, it is assumed that Y_m in 1965 would be equivalent to his 1960 income adjusted by the appropriate age-income

index values and an annual 3.4 percent productivity
increase. This estimated Y_m is then used to compute a value comparable to Y_e. To differentiate
this value from Y_e it is designated Y_e^*. Thus the
total <u>increase</u> in expected future lifetime income
is Y_e^*.

The extent to which any given SMSA, B, is increasing the expected future lifetime income of migrants from any given regional commission area, A,
is measured by the term

$$M_{AB} = \frac{\sum_{j=1}^{n} Y_{ej}^{AB} - Y_{ej}^{*AB}}{P_B}$$

where n is the number of migrants and P_B is the
SMSA population.

A comment is in order here on the division of
total income gains to migrants by population of the
migration center. For some purposes, for example,
one may wish to divide the numerator by the total
number of migrants from A to B, which would yield
an index of the average gain in income per migrant.
The problem with this approach in the present context would be that B may be receiving only a few
migrants from A; even though these few may experience relatively high income gains, the relevance of
the receiving center to the lagging area may not be
very important. The way the M_{AB} index is con-
structed, if the migration flow from A to B is dou-
bled (with the same average gain in income per migrant), then the index value would double. This is
as it should be because we are attempting to measure the <u>total</u> impact of a place on the people from
a lagging area. Of course it might be argued that
if our concern is focused on total income gains to
migrants there is no need to use a deflator.

The rationale for the population deflator is
based on the nature of growth-center policy as a
means for helping people in lagging areas. If an
SMSA with 900,000 people is increasing the incomes

of migrants from lagging regions by as much as the
combined totals of three SMSAs, each of which has a
population of 300,000 and each of which is increasing incomes by one-third of the value for the larger
SMSA, the M_{AB} index would yield an equivalent value
for all four SMSAs. In contrast, if one of the
SMSAs with 300,000 inhabitants were increasing total
income of migrants by as much as the SMSA with
900,000 inhabitants, its M_{AB} index would be three
times that of the larger SMSA. This is as it
should be if migration centers are relevant to
growth-center policy, as they are here. The index
indicates to policy makers that, other things being
equal (except population size), a given growth-
center investment is more likely to benefit lagging
region residents if placed in the smaller center
than in the larger center.* It should be noted
that the average and marginal relations between income increase to migrants and population size could
be assumed to be the same. However our arguments
would still hold if, in the example just cited, the
marginal M_{AB} in the smaller center were anywhere
over one-third the average M_{AB} value of the larger
center.

The M_{AB} Rankings

The M_{AB} rankings for the 15 highest-ranking
SMSAs in each region are presented in Table 46.
These SMSAs are by definition migration centers
within the context of this study. Because of sampling errors an SMSA had to receive at least 500
migrants from a given region; i.e., there had to be
at least five migrants in the sample.
The frequency distribution by population-size
class of the 75 migration centers is shown in

---

*The investment is assumed to have the same
effect on employment and population change where-
ever it is placed. Of course external economies
and diseconomies could result in different results
in different places.

TABLE 46

M_{AB} Rankings of Migration Centers, by Regional Commission Areas

SMSA	1960 Population	1970 Population	Percent Change	Est. No. of Migrants from Reg. Commission Area	M_{AB}
Appalachia					
Harrisburg, Pa.	371,653	405,387	9.1	20,100	17.69
Charleston, W.Va.	252,925	224,054	-11.4	11,300	14.62
Knoxville, Tenn.	368,080	391,974	6.5	20,600	14.51
Steubenville-Weirton, O.-W.Va.	167,756	166,385	-0.8	4,800	14.25
Huntsville, Ala.	153,861	224,217	45.7	6,800	14.20
Greenville, S.C.	255,806	294,220	15.0	11,700	13.99
Altoona, Pa.	137,270	134,142	-2.3	2,600	11.96
Greensboro-High Point-Winston-Salem, N.C.	520,249	598,905	15.1	9,600	11.10
Binghamton, N.Y.-Pa.	283,600	297,959	5.1	5,600	9.93
Gadsden, Ala.	96,980	92,430	-4.7	2,400	9.78
Atlanta, Ga.	1,017,188	1,373,629	35.0	24,000	8.53
Jackson, Miss.	221,367	252,713	14.2	3,500	6.67
Chattanooga, Tenn.	283,169	293,034	3.5	6,000	6.64
Muncie, Ind.	110,938	127,861	15.3	1,100	6.40
Lexington, Ky.	131,906	172,927	31.1	3,800	6.29
Coastal Plains					
Raleigh, N.C.	169,082	225,634	33.4	6,300	9.03
Atlanta, Ga.	1,017,188	1,373,629	35.0	19,500	7.13
Augusta, Ga.-S.C.	216,639	249,842	15.3	3,600	6.94
Albany, Ga.	75,680	88,705	17.2	2,700	6.79
Durham, N.C.	154,965	188,786	21.8	2,800	6.68
Greensboro-High Point-Winston-Salem, N.C.	520,249	598,905	15.1	6,600	6.50
Wilmington, N.C.	92,020	103,556	12.5	1,900	5.25
Tallahassee, Fla.	74,225	102,530	38.1	800	5.09
Columbia, S.C.	260,828	315,216	20.9	6,000	4.90
Savannah, Ga.	188,299	182,959	-2.8	3,700	4.77
Charlotte, N.C.	316,781	405,976	28.2	6,800	4.00
Macon, Ga.	180,403	201,108	11.5	2,500	3.22
Greenville, S.C.	255,806	294,220	15.0	4,000	2.70
Jacksonville, Fla.	455,411	513,439	12.7	4,300	2.67
West Palm Beach, Fla.	228,106	345,553	51.5	1,400	2.55
Upper Great Lakes					
Minneapolis-St. Paul, Minn.	1,482,030	1,805,081	21.8	24,800	6.85
Green Bay, Wis.	125,082	157,299	25.8	1,700	6.64
Madison, Wis.	222,095	287,501	29.4	3,100	6.46
Saginaw, Mich.	190,752	217,787	14.2	1,300	6.12
Bay City, Mich.	107,042	116,628	9.0	800	4.99
Muskegon, Mich.	149,943	156,077	4.1	1,000	4.97
Milwaukee, Wis.	1,278,850	1,393,260	8.9	8,600	4.66

142

SMSA	1960 Population	1970 Population	Percent Change	Est. No. of Migrants from Reg. Commission Area	M_{AB}
Upper Great Lakes					
Lansing, Mich.	298,949	373,474	24.9	2,700	3.42
Kenosha, Wis.	100,615	116,734	16.0	500	3.17
Grand Rapids, Mich.	461,907	535,702	16.0	3,200	2.94
Duluth-Superior, Minn.-Wis.	276,596	261,963	-5.3	5,500	2.93
Racine, Wis.	141,781	171,218	20.8	1,200	2.50
Fargo-Moorhead, N.D.-Minn.	106,027	118,555	11.8	1,000	2.46
Flint, Mich.	416,239	493,402	18.5	1,900	2.25
Ann Arbor, Mich.	172,440	230,128	33.5	800	2.20
Ozarks					
Oklahoma City, Okla.	511,833	623,592	21.8	10,900	7.46
Little Rock, Ark.	271,936	315,375	16.0	6,200	6.39
Tulsa, Okla.	418,974	471,743	12.6	6,700	4.47
Kansas City, Mo.-Kan.	1,092,545	1,240,575	13.5	8,500	3.12
Fort Smith, Ark.	135,110	156,750	16.0	2,500	3.05
Texarkana, Tex.-Ark.	91,657	99,411	8.5	700	2.20
Pine Bluff, Ark.	81,373	83,357	2.4	1,400	2.07
Lubbock, Tex.	156,271	175,757	12.5	500	2.02
Wichita, Kan.	381,626	385,994	1.1	2,800	1.79
Topeka, Kan.	141,286	153,687	8.8	900	1.60
New Orleans, La.	907,123	1,034,316	14.0	1,600	1.48
St. Louis, Mo.-Ill.	2,104,669	2,331,016	10.8	7,500	1.33
Rockford, Ill.	230,091	269,829	17.3	600	1.17
Dallas, Tex.	1,119,410	1,539,372	37.5	3,900	0.98
Fort Worth, Tex.	573,215	757,105	32.1	900	0.71
Four Corners					
Salt Lake City, Utah	447,795	556,896	24.4	7,800	4.81
Ogden, Utah	110,744	124,035	12.0	700	3.34
Colorado Springs, Colo.	143,742	228,572	59.0	1,700	2.83
Las Vegas, Nev.	127,016	270,045	112.6	1,000	2.63
Phoenix, Ariz.	663,510	963,132	45.2	9,000	2.62
Denver, Colo.	929,383	1,223,142	31.6	11,300	2.50
Albuquerque, N.M.	262,199	313,829	19.7	4,800	1.90
Tulsa, Okla.	418,974	471,743	12.6	900	0.98
Anaheim-Santa Ana-Garden Grove, Cal.	703,925	1,409,335	100.2	1,400	0.85
Tucson, Ariz.	265,660	344,904	29.8	1,900	0.84
Pueblo, Colo.	118,707	117,212	-1.3	800	0.80
Amarillo, Tex.	149,493	140,876	-5.8	900	0.75
El Paso, Tex.	314,070	355,919	13.3	1,300	0.65
Dallas, Tex.	1,119,410	1,539,372	37.5	2,100	0.65
San Diego, Cal.	1,033,011	1,318,022	27.6	1,400	0.63

Table 47. The χ^2 value computed from the observed
frequencies and the frequencies that would be expected on the basis of the distribution of all the
nation's SMSAs was 3.53--not significant even at
the 50 percent level. Thus the analyses and policy
suggestions that follow are consistent with the
nature of the nation's relatively stable urban
hierarchy. In other words, whereas some popular
policy proposals to attain more so-called balanced
growth in the country emphasize measures to force-
feed growth in smaller cities and rural areas, this
is not our intent.

TABLE 47

Frequency Distribution of Migration
Centers, by Population Size, 1970

Population Size	Frequency	Relative Frequency
Less than 100,000	5	.07
100,000-199,999	19	.25
200,000-499,999	31	.41
500,000-749,999	6	.08
750,000-999,999	2	.03
1,000,000 and over	12	.16
Totals	75	1.00

It should also be noted that Appalachian centers account for 14 of the 25 highest M_{AB} values.
However this does not imply that the Appalachian
centers are more efficient than the others. Rather
the high proportion reflects differences in population size and therefore in potential number of migrants. In 1960 the Appalachian region had a population of 15,328,000, whereas the four other regions had a combined population of only 11,434,000.*

*Taking the three highest-ranking centers in
each case, the average M_{AB} value for Appalachia is

MIGRATION CENTERS AS GROWTH CENTERS

The data in Table 48 show that when considering the 15 highest-ranking migration centers for
each regional commission area, 40 of the 75 migration centers grew at a faster rate than the nation's
SMSA population, which grew by 15.1 percent over
the decade. However, when only the Title V commissions are considered, it is seen that each had a
higher proportion of fast-growing migration centers
than did Appalachia, ranging from 40 percent in the
case of the Ozarks to 73 percent in the case of the
coastal plains. In all, 60 percent of the Title V
centers grew by more than the weighted national
average, whereas only 27 percent of the Appalachian
centers fell into this category.

The contrast between the Title V commissions
and Appalachia is even more striking when only the
five highest-ranking migration centers for each region are considered. No less than three of the
five centers are fast-growing in each Title V region, with a total of 75 percent falling into this
category. Indeed, eight of the nine highest-ranking
coastal plains centers are fast-growing, as are six
of the seven highest-ranking Four Corners centers.
The five highest-ranking Ozarks centers all grew by
over 12 percent, and the three highest-ranking upper Great Lakes centers grew by over 20 percent.
In marked contrast only one of the five top-ranking
Appalachian migration centers--Huntsville--was
fast-growing, while two actually lost population.

15.61; for the coastal plains, 7.70; for the upper
Great Lakes, 6.65; for the Ozarks, 6.11; and for
the Four Corners, 3.66. The respective 1960 populations of these regions (in millions) were 15.33,
4.49, 2.69, 2.50, and 1.76. This correspondence
can be seen by comparing the average M_{AB} values for
the highest-ranked centers when $n > 3$ for each region. It should be noted, however, that a correlation coefficient would tend to overstate the degree
of association because of the relatively high values
of Appalachia on both the abscissa and the ordinate.

TABLE 48

Number of Migration Centers Growing Faster
than the National Average, 1960-70, among
the Fifteen and Five Highest-Ranking
Migration Centers for Regional
Commission Areas

Area	Among Fifteen Highest-Ranking	Among Five Highest-Ranking
Coastal plains	11	5
Four Corners	10	4
Ozarks	6	3
Upper Great Lakes	9	3
Title V total	36	15
Appalachia	4	1
Grand total	40	16

Source: U.S. Bureau of Census, U.S. Census of
Population: 1970, Number of Inhabitants, Final Re-
port PC(1)-AI, United States Summary (Washington,
D.C., 1971).

Of the ten highest-ranking Appalachian migration
centers, only Huntsville exceeded the national SMSA
growth rate by more than one percentage point, while
four lost population.

These results indicate that, where the Title V
commissions are concerned, there is a pronounced
tendency for migration centers to be population
growth centers, but that this is definitely not the
case for Appalachia.

SPATIAL DISTRIBUTION OF MIGRATION CENTERS

The data in Table 49 show the distribution of
migration centers between regional commission and
nonregional commission areas of states that have
regional commission areas. Once again it is necessary to consider the Title V regions and Appalachia separately.

TABLE 49

SMSAs and Migration Centers in Regional Commission and
Nonregional Commission Areas of Relevant States

Area	Relevant States		Regional Commission Areas		Nonregional Commission Areas	
	Total SMSAs	Total Migration Centers	Total SMSAs	Total Migration Centers	Total SMSAs	Total Migration Centers
Coastal plains	16	12	10	7	6	5
Four Corners	9	8	4	3	5	5
Ozarks	12	10	3	2	9	8
Upper Great Lakes	18	15	3	3	15	12
Title V total	55	45	20	15	35	30
Appalachia	69	14	19	10	50	4

Source: U.S. Bureau of the Census, U.S. Census of Population: 1970, Number of Inhabitants, Final Report PC(1)-AI, United States Summary (Washington, D.C., 1971).

The Title V regions taken together have twice
as many (30 to 15) migration centers in the nonregional commission portions of the relevant states
as in the commission areas. In addition a higher
proportion of the SMSAs in nonregional commission
areas are migration centers (86 percent to 75 percent). The coastal plains, Four Corners, and Ozarks
regions each have a higher proportion of migration
centers in the noncommission portions; and 12 of
the 15 SMSAs in Michigan, Wisconsin, and Minnesota
outside of the upper Great Lakes region are among
the 15 highest-ranking migration centers for the
upper Great Lakes.

Another indication of the importance of non-
commission-area SMSAs in the relevant states is
that, of the 24 migration centers made up of the 6
highest-ranking centers from each Title V region,
15 are outside the regions but in the relevant
states. Of the 15, 13 grew by 12 percent or more
between 1960 and 1970, and 10 grew more than the
national average.

Appalachia again is an exception: 14 of the
15 migration centers are in the Appalachian states,
but, in contrast to the Title V regions, 10 lie
within Appalachia and only 4 are in other parts of
the 13 relevant states. Slightly over one-half of
the Appalachian SMSAs were migration centers, but
this was the case for only 8 percent of the non-
Appalachian SMSAs in the relevant states.*

Looked at another way, if one were to take the
17 highest-ranking migration centers for Appalachia,

----

*The Appalachian states have 69 SMSAs, more
than the combined Title V states. Still, if one
were to take the 60 highest-ranking Appalachian migration centers (rather than 15), 18 of the 19 SMSAs
in Appalachia would be migration centers. But this
would be the case for only 25 of the 50 SMSAs in
nonregional commission areas of the Appalachian
states. About one-third of the top 60 migration
centers would lie outside of the 13 Appalachian
states.

12 are in the region proper. Of these 12, 6 are
losing population and 3 others grew by less than
half the national SMSA average. In contrast, the
4 centers outside of Appalachia but still within
the 13 relevant stages grew by 9.1, 14.2, 31.1 and
35.0 percent. Thus, while Appalachians are increasing their incomes by moving into SMSAs within
the Appalachian region, the long-run prospects of
the places into which they are moving are often at
best stagnant. Thus, as a general tendency, the
migration centers relevant to the Title V commissions would be naturally consistent with a growth
center policy oriented toward people from lagging
regions, but the Appalachian migration centers
would not.

SUMMARY AND POLICY IMPLICATIONS

It has been recognized for some time that one
of the potential problems with the planning done
by most of the regional commissions up to this
point is that it has been planning for only a portion of a state. This may result in cases where
the desire for region-wide plans conflicts with the
effort to develop statewide approaches. This could
easily create additional problems in terms of data
collection, coordination at both the state and federal levels,and the accountability of elected officials.[5]
Apart from political and administrative difficulties, the present study indicates that the current regional commission approach of working primarily within lagging portions of states is not
economically efficient, at least insofar as policy
is concerned with people rather than places. The
results show that the most efficient migration cen-
ters--in terms of increasing the incomes of migrants
from lagging areas--tend to be outside of the lagging areas but not big, distant cities. Instead
they tend to be growth centers in the nonregional
commission portions of the relevant states.
The legislation that created the regional commissions called for a growth-center strategy to

take advantage of potential growth opportunities
for lagging region residents. The analysis presented here supports the growth-center strategy but
suggests that the regional commission approach
should be based on whole states. Revenue-sharing
with the states may also be preferable to the present regional commission approach, although it could
be implemented through a redefined regional commission system based on whole states. The important
point is that the problems of people in lagging regions need to be dealt with in a larger geographic
perspective than that of the lagging regions themselves.

It was suggested earlier in this book that it
would be more efficient from both a national viewpoint and the preferences of many potential migrants
in lagging areas to give more emphasis to comprehensive relocation assistance in the mix of public
policies affecting spatial resource allocation.
The importance of intrastate moves means that governors could actively support comprehensive voluntary relocation assistance programs within a regional commission and/or revenue-sharing framework
without having to fear losing population to other
states.

Finally the exceptional nature of Appalachia
must be noted. It is more difficult to generalize
with respect to this region because it is so much
larger than any of the Title V commission areas.
(The Appalachian Regional Commission has itself
divided the area into four fairly distinct sub-
regions.) Nevertheless while there is significant
movement out of Appalachia to migration centers
that are also growth centers in the non-Appalachian
portions of the 13 relevant states, there is an
even stronger tendency for Appalachian movers to
move to migration centers within Appalachia. However these Appalachian SMSAs are generally declining or stagnant. Thus while federal policies based
on growth centers and comprehensive relocation
assistance could build on existing migration patterns in the Title V states, the Appalachian case
would seem to call for greater efforts to redirect
migration streams in favor of "outside" growth

centers. It may be suggested that a few pilot
training and relocation projects be attempted in
this regard, financed perhaps out of some of the
relatively plentiful funds that federal development
agencies now devote to road and sewer projects in
areas whose most critical problems lie in the do-
main of human resource development.

6

A CONCLUDING
PERSPECTIVE

Although this book has been primarily concerned
with location preferences and migration within the
context of relatively poor areas, it would, of
course, be misleading to give the impression that
rural areas and small towns are generally no longer
viable. Indeed during the 1960s there were approximately 200 nonmetropolitan area towns with populations of between 10,000 and 50,000 that grew by 15
percent or more, while the corresponding rate for
the country as a whole was 13 percent.[1] About half
of these towns were located in the South. The reasons for their relatively rapid growth were of
course quite varied, but two of their most common
characteristics were location on the National Interstate Highway system and the presence of a college
or university. Similarly there were nearly 500
counties that had lost population during the 1950s
but gained during the 1960s. This phenomenon was
most prevalent in upland areas of the South, particularly in northern and western Arkansas and in
eastern Oklahoma. Another noteworthy area in this
regard was the lower Tennessee valley.

On the other hand about 1,350 counties--well
over a third of the national total--had such heavy
outmigration during the 1960s that they experienced
absolute population declines. About 500 counties
had fewer births than deaths in 1970 because so many
young adults had left; in 1960 there were only 38
such counties, and in 1950 only two! There also

were approximately 300 counties that gained population in the 1950s but lost population in the 1960s.
The Great Plains had heavy outmigration from the
Dakotas down into Texas.   There were seven contigu-
ous states from Idaho through the northern plains
to Minnesota and Iowa in which most counties had net
outmigration and frequently absolute decline.

There are those who view population loss as
such with alarm; in fact numerous bills are before
Congress to provide special assistance to these
"distressed" areas.   However it is difficult to com-
pare the situation in the Plains, the upper Great
Lakes, northern New England, and other relatively
prosperous areas with relatively heavy outmigration
to the situation in poorer areas.   In the Plains,
for example, outmigrants have generally been well
prepared to take advantage of economic opportunities
in other areas.   Of course the population left behind has a relatively high proportion of older
people, and it is often difficult to maintain essential services for a widely dispersed population.
On the other hand agriculture is viable and there
is little poverty.   In addition to savings and farm
income there is considerable income from the federal
government in the form of farm subsidies and Social
Security benefits.   There are also viable small
towns, though they probably should be developed as
service centers for rural hinterlands rather than
as growth centers capable of halting and even reversing outmigration.   Economic theory maintains
that outmigration should raise the marginal product
of the remaining labor force, other things being
equal.   And, in fact, the evidence indicates that
population adjustments in the Plains reflect successful adaptations not only for outmigrants but
for the people left behind.   The greatest acceleration of nonmetropolitan income in the county has
taken place in the Plains, rising from a rate of
change of 2.9 percent in the 1950s to 6.2 percent
in the 1960s.   Thus our principal concern is with
problems stemming from rural poverty.

RURAL POVERTY

While it is clear that millions of farm people
need or will need training and preparation for nonfarm work and modes of life, their adaptation is
often strained by poverty and all of its unfortunate
attributes. Poverty levels have been defined on the
basis of a modified Social Security definition by a
federal agency committee so that such factors as
family size, sex of the family head, number of children under 18 years old, and farm-nonfarm residence,
can be taken into account. The weighted average
poverty level threshold in 1970 for a nonfarm family
of four was $3,968, whereas that for a comparable
farm family was $3,385. In that year the total num-
ber of persons in farm families below the poverty
level was 436,000. This represented 18.6 percent
of the farm population, or about twice as high as
the 9.6 percent of nonfarm persons below the poverty
level.

The data in Table 50 show the number and proportion of poverty-status persons in 1969 by type of
residence. The number of persons below the poverty
level was about the same in metropolitan and nonmetropolitan areas, but the proportion in nonmetropolitan areas was about twice as high. The poverty
of the Negro population is striking, particularly
in nonmetropolitan areas. Whereas about 25 percent
of the metropolitan Negroes were below the poverty
level (contrary to the situation among whites, there
is little difference between the central city and
suburbs), more than 50 percent of those in nonmetropolitan areas were in poverty status.

It should be pointed out that although the pool
of potential rural-to-urban migrants is less than
formerly, problems of urban slums cannot be divorced
from problems of rural poverty. Data for 1967 indicate that rural migrants to central cities were more
likely to live in poverty areas than were nonmigrants
or persons who had migrated from other urban areas.
This was especially true for blacks; fully two-thirds
of the black rural-to-urban migrants in central
cities were in poverty areas.[2]

TABLE 50

Persons by Poverty Status, by Type of Residence, 1969

Residence Type	All Races Total ('000)	All Races Below Poverty Level Number ('000)	All Races Percent of Total	White Total ('000)	White Below Poverty Level Number ('000)	White Percent of Total	Negro Total ('000)	Negro Below Poverty Level Number ('000)	Negro Percent of Total
United States	199,849	24,289	12.2	175,231	16,668	9.5	22,349	7,214	32.3
Metropolitan	130,017	12,320	9.5	112,440	8,200	7.3	15,824	3,855	24.4
Central city	57,781	7,760	13.4	44,392	4,527	10.2	12,439	3,068	24.7
Metro ring	72,236	4,560	6.3	68,049	3,674	5.4	3,384	786	23.2
Nonmetropolitan	69,831	11,969	17.1	62,791	8,468	13.5	6,525	3,359	51.5

Source: U.S. Bureau of the Census, "Consumer Income," Current Population Reports, Series P-60, No. 76, table 3.

Finally, workers employed in agriculture and in small businesses in rural areas tend to be relatively deprived in terms of the protections afforded by social legislation, such as unemployment compensation, Workmen's Compensation, union organization if they wish, welfare safeguards, and minimum wage and overtime guarantees. As Vernon Briggs has pointed out:

> Regardless of race, anyone who is employed in the agricultural sector is a second-class citizen. For although large farm owners are the most privileged group in American corporate society (with import quota protection; anti-trust exemptions; price supports; soil bank purchases; subsidized research, irrigation, land reclamation, and erosion projects; and special property tax rates), farm workers survive only by the law of the jungle. In no sector is Michael Harrington's famous thesis that the welfare state has brought the benefits of socialism to the rich and the horrors of laissez-faire to the poor more vividly exemplified.[3]

The many public policy measures that have been implemented on behalf of rural areas have undoubtedly resulted in widespread benefits to rural people. However economic analysis focuses not simply on the benefits of undertakings but also on the costs. To the economist the cost of using scarce resources in a particular way is the best foregone use of these resources. One has to choose and something must be given up. So in examining the policies and programs affecting rural areas it is necessary to consider what opportunities have been lost, as well as what benefits have been gained. Here some hard questions must be posed concerning rural development objectives.

It is assumed, for example, in some regional development legislation that the unemployment of an area can be reduced by measures designed to increase

employment. However, as George Iden has shown, "except for extreme cases, the unemployment level is
not closely related to the growth characteristics
of the area." There are many areas of persistent
high unemployment that also have rates of population increase, employment growth, net inmigration,
and labor force participation rates similar to the
corresponding averages for all areas.[4] Similarly a
recent study found that 36 percent of the nation's
counties with an employment growth rate at or above
the national average between 1950 and 1960 had an
increase of one or more percentage points in their
county unemployment rates. Thus it is evident that
growth factors must be considered along with unemployment rates before determining that an area is
lagging and therefore in need of aid.[5]

Considerable attention should be given to who
benefits from policies designed to increase an
area's employment; regional subsidies may actually
result in job leakages that keep the poor at or
near the same income level even though average incomes may be increasing. An analysis of industrialization in the Ozarks found that "migrants tended to
intervene between jobs and the rural poor who would
be targets for an industrialization program."[6] It
concludes that, although industrialization can be a
major component of a poverty policy, from the perspective of the unskilled rural poor in the Ozarks,
the strength of the approach needs to be improved
with auxiliary measures.[7]

The emphasis that has been given to employment
growth has frequently tended to shroud the more general problem of raising per capita incomes in rural
America. It was pointed out earlier that underem-
ployment rather than unemployment appears to be the
principal contributor to the relatively low economic
status of many rural residents. A major cause of
relatively low rural incomes, apart from the problem
of agricultural employment, is the nature of the
jobs that tend to become available in rural areas.
Wilbur Thompson argues that:

> In national perspective, industries
> filter down through the system of

cities, from places of greater to
lesser industrial sophistication.
Most often, the highest skills are
needed in the difficult, early stage
of mastering a new process, and
skill requirements decline steadily
as the production process is ration-
alized and routinized with experience.
As the industry slides down the learn-
ing curve, the high wage rates of the
more industrially sophisticated inno-
vating areas become superfluous. The
aging industry seeks out industrial
backwaters where the cheaper labor is
now up to the lesser demands of the
simplified process.[8]

And it is, of course, small towns and rural
areas that constitute the lowest rung of the filter-
ing process. Until they are able to capture firms
earlier in the life cycles of industries, they will
continue--in all too many cases--to run along the
treadmill of trading dying industries for low-skill,
low-wage mature industries.

It has been shown in Chapter 1 that discussions
of policies for upgrading the economic status of
rural areas and some legislation in this regard
often cite the objective of more so-called balanced
growth for the nation, but that this term does not
in itself provide much in the way of concrete objectives. It would be unfortunate if the balanced
growth argument were simply to be used as a code
expression for spending more money in rural areas
per se. There may be good reasons for subsidizing
industrialists and plantation owners, but presumably
our major concern is with helping disadvantaged
people. Many agricultural and rural development
policies appear to be less concerned with objectives
directly related to disadvantaged people than with
place-oriented objectives whose benefits may never
reach the disadvantaged.

Finally even the strongest supporters of rural
development would be loathe to argue that all rural
areas are economically viable or equally deserving

of development funds. Efforts to develop growth
centers in rural areas are implicitly based on the
notion that a certain amount of geographically concentrated economic activity is desirable. However
there has been some confusion of the growth-center
notion with that of service centers. A small town
or city may be developed as a service center for its
rural hinterland without its actually becoming a
growth center in terms of population and employment.
In any case a somewhat different approach must be
taken in thinking through the objectives of public
policy for growth and service centers. Service-
center analysis is best undertaken within the theoretical framework of central place theory and the
urban hierarchy. Growth-center analysis, on the
other hand, needs to be more dynamic. It must be
admitted, however, that growth-center theory is
still in a very imperfect state.[9]

URBAN ALTERNATIVES TO RURAL POVERTY

In contrast to rural development advocates,
many authorities emphasize the advantages of larger
urban areas. Alexander Ganz argues that the economies of big cities are showing new strength and a
larger potential. "Our studies," Ganz writes, "show
that despite all of the limitations of life in the
ghetto, non-white labor forces migrating to the large
cities are experiencing notable gains in wages and
earnings. The absorption and upgrading of this disadvantaged population is a national problem and a
national task which the cities are performing."[10]
Thus he urges that

> Federal policy should be explicitly
> designed to favor the large cities
> and their ghettos through expendi-
> ture, grant, loan guarantee and regu-
> latory programs, in accordance with a
> measure of their need and their po-
> tential contribution to national
> growth and welfare. Federal policy
> has recently begun to move in this

direction on a number of fronts, but
an explicit policy determination
would help assure that Federal policy
would no longer work at cross purposes.[11]

In a similar vein William Alonso, citing evidence from this country and elsewhere that income
rises sharply with urban size,[12] finds that an
urban-rural balance policy "appears highly questionable on the grounds of its feasibility, its impact,
and its consequences."[13] Migration from the country
to the cities, he argues, is a worldwide phenomenon
associated with economic and social advance. Moreover, because only 5 percent of the growth of metropolitan areas is attributable to net migration from
nonmetropolitan areas (80 percent is due to natural
increase and 13 percent to international migration),
the impact of migration reversal would not be very
significant for the big cities--though it could be
for some rural areas--because of their small population base. Steering manufacturing to the country-
side may improve local economic health, but there
would be some mixture of blessings. Most plants
would be branch plants dependent on distant corpo-
rate headquarters, and many would be marginal operations attracted by subsidies. From a manpower viewpoint, Alonso finds that "in the towns or dispersed
agro-industrial communities, there would be the
limitations of career choices and advancement opportunities and the danger of unemployment which char-
acterizes such small economies."[14] Brian Berry is
even more explicit. On the basis of national studies of numerous welfare indicators, he argues that
"proper regional strategies" will only be possible
"when regional economic development policies are explicitly urban in orientation, urban in content,
urban in result. To try to keep people down on the
farm, or in the small town, is to condemn regional
policy to failure."[15]

It is noteworthy that the arguments advanced
by advocates of the big city seldom take account of
the unquantifiable social costs of urban congestion.
If data limitations preclude our making the relevant

subtractions from private pecuniary gain to firms
and individuals, it is still unwise simply to ignore
these problems. If big cities have so many net advantages over other areas, it is curious that the
poll results reported in Chapter 3 show such a
marked preference for nonmetropolitan areas. Of
course the condition of job availability is critical, and, as Wilbur Thompson has pointed out,

> If blue-collar, middle-income workers
> should happen to prefer small towns
> or medium-size cities as places to
> live and to fish, such a preference
> is irrelevant as a locational factor.
> What could be most relevant is that
> the wives of corporate managers pre-
> fer the theater. Under unionism
> [i.e., equal wages in all places],
> managers become increasingly free to
> locate where they would like to live.[16]

Thompson and others who emphasize the importance of
urban amenities assume that management will always
tend to locate in big cities. Until recently this
has been true, but now there is mounting evidence
that the managers who determine where the workers
will live are increasingly inclined to shun the big
city.[17]

On the other hand there is another bias in
favor of large urban areas resulting from the asym-
metry of migration. Thompson points out that while
the relatively young and better educated do frequently move to big cities because they prefer them,
"With time and aging, many come to favor the environment of smaller places, but the elderly tend not
to move easily due to heavy sunk investments in
homes, friends and local institutions and due also
to the shorter remaining life over which the money
and psychic cost of moving must be recaptured."[18]
Moreover, by simply not moving, many people "choose"
a larger place as a consequence of the long-term
growth of places that were once not large. In general, then, there is a bias toward bigness "because
those who prefer large cities do tend to act on

those preferences and those who prefer smaller places
tend not to act. Note also that this age-bias tends
to reinforce the 'skill-bias' in migration . . .
through which professional and technical workers lock
the semi-skilled production workers into their locational preferences for larger urban places."[19]

In contrast to the proponents of rural development and the defenders of the big city, our own approach has been to emphasize the importance of
intermediate-sized cities as growth centers. This
approach also puts more stress on movement of people
from lagging areas to growth centers than on spread
effects from growth centers to lagging hinterlands.
Big cities on the one hand and small towns and rural
areas on the other obviously need and will receive a
great deal of public investment. But there do not
seem to be persuasive reasons for singling either
group out for special favor--especially when growing
intermediate-sized cities offer more opportunities
in terms of existing external economies than do
small towns and rural areas and fewer diseconomies
than do large metropolitan areas. And if there is
planned growth of intermediate-sized cities with
relevance to the populations of lagging regions,
then these growth centers can be provided with an
integrated and coherent system of public overhead
capital in advance of demand. Of course a growth
center need not be limited to one city. A system
of cities and towns linked by adequate transportation and communications could serve as well or better. And such a system could take the form of a
cluster of centers or a development axis.

In any case it is increasingly meaningless to
differentiate between rural and urban America. What
is needed is a broader perspective for devising, in-
tegrating, and implementing regional and manpower
policies. This perspective would emphasize fusions
of metropolitan and nonmetropolitan areas as well
as the spatial interdependencies within them. As
Varden Fuller points out:

> We are an urban society; the questions
> for the future are not urban versus
> rural but rather what kind of urban.

> Obviously, the concept implied is not
> density of settlement or distance
> away from a metropolitan center but
> rather the quality of urbaneness in
> the population. Even though the
> hinterlands are likely to remain, it
> is not to be assumed or expected
> that they will (or ought to!) be in-
> habited by hinterlandish people, for
> whom hinterlandish institutions of
> human development are sufficient.[20]

While such concepts as "metropolitan region,"
"spread city," "megalopolis," "commuting field,"
"functional economic area," and "consolidated urban
region" have been suggested to describe this phenomenon, I prefer the term "urban field," which has been
defined in the following terms:

> Looking ahead to the next generation,
> we foresee a new scale of urban liv-
> ing that will extend far beyond exist-
> ing metropolitan cores and penetrate
> deeply into the periphery. Relations
> of dominance and dependency will be
> transcended. The older established
> centers, together with the intermetro-
> politan peripheries that envelop them,
> will constitute the new ecological
> unit of America's post-industrial so-
> ciety that will replace traditional
> concepts of the city and metropolis.
> This basic element of the emerging
> spatial order we shall call the
> "urban field."[21]

The notion of an urban field is based on spatial interdependencies within core areas having a
minimum population of 300,000 persons and extending
outwards for approximately 100 miles--that is, a
driving distance of about two hours.[22]
    In the past it has been true that metropolitan
growth has tended to draw off productive population,
investment capital, and economic activities from

many hinterland areas, and in some places this is
still the case. However, Friedmann and Miller have
argued that there are now indications that the urbanization process may be reversing this trend. In
the future, they maintain, centrifugal forces may
propel the settlement of population and economic activity from existing metropolitan centers into the
present hinterland. The hinterland has space, scen-
ery, and communities that are increasingly attractive to metropolitan populations. Demand for these
resources is being generated by rising real income,
increasing leisure, and increasing mobility. Moreover new technologies will probably make it more
possible to relax the need for physical proximity
in distribution, marketing, information services,
and decision-making. For example, computerized
business inventory systems, videophones, and the
use of coded cards to send information, order items,
and transfer funds by telephone will make possible
greater decentralization of business activities.
Improvements in transportation technology will continue to shrink distances and to improve accessibil-
ity. When the National Interstate Highway system
is complete, an estimated 3.5-7.5 million acres
will be opened up for development. The combined impact of these and similar forces are and will be
leading to uses of the "rural" hinterland for purposes that are "urban" in character. While the
older metropolitan cores may continue to be the centers for major educational and government institutions, famous museums, and outstanding cultural and
sports events, many activities can be decentralized
through the urban field.

This approach may appear overly drawn in view
of the external economies that continue to exert a
strong pull toward urban centers. There is, for
example, a strong hint of the "tourism" cry that
too often is the last gasp of a dying area. Tourism and related recreation activities have few important linkages with other industries and the
skill requirements they demand are generally low.

The importance of the extension of the National
Interstate Highway system to many rural areas also
should not be exaggerated. For example, a recent

study by Kuehn and West indicates that highways have
not been a basic factor in the economic development
of the Ozarks region. They conclude that "Success
in economic development efforts is not assured by
construction of more and better highways," and that
"the probability of success is dependent on the existence of prior dynamism in the region. The investment in highways must be part of a cluster of
change."[23] This finding is consistent with those
of other investigators.[24]

     Nevertheless there is evidence of emerging de-
centralization around larger nonmetropolitan centers,
though different regions of the country have different patterns. A smaller proportion of larger incorporated places of the nonmetropolitan United States
over 2,500 population grew in the 1960s compared to
the previous decade, but in the South and North-
Central regions there was an increase in the proportion of smaller places growing. There is still an
overall prevailing pattern of greater growth in
larger nonmetropolitan centers, and places near
large cities are more likely to grow than those in
more remote locations. Within the SMSAs, however,
there is a very low or even inverse relationship between size and growth, indicating the presence of a
decentralization process.[25] Fuguitt suggests that

> this is because centers near metropoli-
> tan centers may grow in population as
> part of a decentralization process, be-
> coming commuter towns or new homes of
> industry. Within such an extended
> metropolitan community, residential
> and commercial location decisions may
> be influenced less by factors directly
> associated with size of place as by
> such things as the availability of
> space for housing, tax structure,
> quality of schools, etc.--considera-
> tions which might actually be more
> favorable in smaller centers.[26]

In the South there appears to be considerable decentralization even beyond the SMSAs. There the

proportion of small places growing increased in the
1960s relative to the 1950s, regardless of location
with respect to the SMSAs. This is consistent with
a number of studies indicating that metropolitan
and nonmetropolitan areas in the South are both
sharing significantly in employment growth in non-
primary industries.[27]

Given that patterns of growth and changes in
growth reveal interdependencies among nonmetropolitan places as well as between them and the larger
SMSAs, Fuguitt concludes that there is a need to
view individual places

> within the context of their position
> within systems of larger and smaller
> population centers, and their area
> setting. This tends to support growth
> center strategy for encouraging eco-
> nomic and population growth, but there
> is no agreement on the size of the
> growth center that should be encour-
> aged, and with it, the size of the
> rural region presumed to benefit.
> Practical politics, with the large
> number of small governmental units in
> rural areas, makes it very difficult
> to designate one center over another,
> or to concentrate attention only on
> larger places. Similar considerations
> make it difficult not to concentrate
> attention on the poorer areas and
> places (termed by Hansen the "worst
> first" policy), despite the agrument
> given by economists to turn first to
> places giving the most promise of
> moving into a process of sustained
> growth.
>   The need to look beyond the in-
> dividual place in seeking to influence
> population distribution is recognized
> currently at the local level with the
> so-called multicounty area.[28]

Numerous federal agencies have created their
own multicounty organizations in order to broaden

the geographic scope of their planning. While this
may make each agency's activities more efficient in
terms of its own means and ends, the proliferation
of such groups has led to severe overlapping and
duplication. Indeed there are now more multicounty
planning groups than there are counties! Because
most proposals for financing rural development rec-
ognize the importance of multicounty planning, it
is essential that federal, state, and local governments agree on uniform boundaries for multicounty
planning groups. The Intergovernmental Cooperation
Act of 1968 and Circular A-95 of the Office of Management and Budget represent important steps forward
in this regard. Although some states, e.g., Texas,
Oregon, and Georgia, have made noteworthy strides in
implementing effective multicounty planning schemes,
the national picture as a whole still leaves much to
be desired. (The Texas system is particularly interesting in the present context because each planning region has a metropolitan core.) It would seem
that progress in this regard depends in large measure on state governors. Eichner correctly points
out that "the ability of the individual states to
affect economic development is far greater than is
usually appreciated. Even though the ultimate
source of the funds may be the federal government,
the fact is that the states are the principal mechanism by which government expenditures for domestic
purposes are made."[29] But the governors must create
meaningful planning units and compel the various
federal agencies to coordinate their plans, programs,
and projects within the frameworks that they establish. Rural areas have difficulties enough without
having to endure inefficiencies of piecemeal and un-
coordinated planning efforts.
    Whether development financing efforts will be
based on block grants, revenue sharing, regional
commissions, special development banks, tax incentives, or some combination of these means, multicounty planning units must be imaginative and inno-
vative if they are to convert financial advantages--
which permit economic development but do not guaran-
tee it--into real capital expansion in hinterland
areas. Local industrial development corporations
may be useful, but they must make some hard choices

in the light of realistic assessments of area resources and growth potentials. Careful decisions
must be made concerning what resources to devote to
public works investment to create an attractive infrastructure on the one hand, and direct financial
subsidies to private firms on the other. It may be
desirable to improve the quality of services to an
area's people, but programs in this regard should
not be confused with growth-center projects and programs intended to spur economic growth, though there
may, of course, be projects that are appropriate to
simultaneous service-center and growth-center policies.

It is also essential to develop federated local
labor markets with a comprehensive and coordinated
employment service.[30] The need to simulate greater
scale has been emphasized by Wilbur Thompson, who
suggests that:

> A number of small- and medium-size
> urban areas, connected by good high-
> ways and/or rail lines may form a
> loose network of interrelated labor
> markets. With widespread ownership
> of automobiles and a well-developed
> bus system on expressways permitting
> average speeds of 50 miles an hour,
> the effective local labor market would
> extend radially for 25 to 30 miles
> around one of the larger urban places.
> A couple of small cities of, say,
> 25,000 population, with two or three
> main industries each, plus a half-
> dozen small one- or two-industry
> towns of half that size add up to a
> 100,000 to 200,000 population, ex-
> tended local market, built on the
> moderately broad base of more than a
> dozen important industries.[31]

Of course many rural areas may not be able to
mount an effort based on places of this size. Nevertheless they should cooperate to the maximum extent
possible. In addition it should be emphasized that,

in the multicounty development programs I have observed around the country, the poor and disadvantaged have rarely been given an opportunity to benefit from the fruits of economic progress. They
simply have no effective advocacy, and too few pressures exist to give they such advocacy.

Finally the findings presented in this book
suggest that the greatest gap in the mix of public
policies intended to influence the spatial distribution of population and economic activity is the
lack of programs that would give potential migrants
from lagging areas the skills and training to match
job opportunities in intermediate areas, as well as
comprehensive relocation assistance.[32] There is no
question here of "moving people out." In our market
system it is no more possible to compel people to
leave lagging areas than it is possible to compel
industry to move into them. But it is a question
of giving people viable alternatives--and therefore
of giving them the possibility of genuine choice.

Economic Development District	Development Center Personal Income Growth Rate, 1959-68 (%)	Development Center Personal Income Growth Rate, 1950-59 (%)	Development Center Population Size, 1960	Development Center/Hinterland Population Ratio	Hinterland Personal Income Growth Rate, 1959-68 (%)
East, Arkansas	75.8	55.8	21,418	.053400	78.5
Southeast Arkansas	84.6	84.0	44,037	.239900	66.0
Heart of Georgia, Georgia	117.0	60.6	13,814	.153600	91.7
Northeast, Georgia	112.8	93.2	31,355	.274000	90.7
Oconee, Georgia	105.2	84.6	11,117	.133840	81.5
Slash Pine, Georgia	78.4	64.5	20,944	.230600	83.7
Middle Flint, Georgia	126.8	58.6	13,472	.182342	113.0
Clearwater, Idaho	44.9	55.4	12,691	.204500	47.1
Greater Egypt, Illinois	91.1	68.7	14,670	.089300	56.1
West Central, Indiana	63.7	43.2	72,500	.633900	82.7
Fivco, Kentucky	64.2	63.2	31,283	.349900	83.7
Lincoln Trail, Kentucky	107.9	38.7	15,460	.095190	87.2
Capital, Louisiana	81.3	101.8	152,419	.49650	121.8
Evangeline, Louisiana	94.8	108.8	69,462	.20040	95.2
Kisatchie Delta, Louisiana	75.7	80.6	48,915	.23020	183.9
North Delta, Louisiana	86.8	85.4	67,434	.31050	79.6
Northwest, Louisiana	59.7	56.9	197,148	.71140	85.5
Pride, Maine	49.0	76.4	47,921	.22580	60.4
Western Upper, Michigan	86.7	78.4	2,358	.02480	40.5
Arrowhead, Minnesota	58.4	44.9	106,884	.47310	37.2
North Central, Mississippi	108.4	52.2	7,914	.05530	80.0
Ozark Foothills, Missouri	60.0	33.2	15,926	.34930	72.0
South Central Ozark, Missouri	64.0	63.1	5,836	.07164	38.0
North Central, New Mexico	75.5	80.8	33,394	.27310	73.7
Pee Dee, South Carolina	96.0	70.9	21,591	.11635	92.0
Upper Savannah, South Carolina	123.0	20.7	16,644	.12270	84.6
Brazos Valley, Texas	110.0	73.7	38,938	.47580	64.7
Deep East, Texas	85.0	75.2	30,315	.16150	82.8
Low Rio Grande Valley, Texas	66.3	46.7	32,728	.10250	53.2
Lenowisco, Virginia	73.0	45.2	5,390	.05680	68.8

Economic Development District	Development Center: Personal Income Growth Rate, 1959-68 (%)	Development Center: Personal Income Growth Rate, 1950-1959 (%)	Development Center: Population Size, 1960	Development Center/ Hinterland Population Ratio	Hinterland Personal Income Growth Rate, 1959-68 (%)
North Central, Arkansas	127.1	30.8	6,207	.04940	91.2
Northwest, Arkansas	122.1	60.9	30,350	.25380	105.6
West Central, Arkansas	100.0	31.1	28,337	.20190	101.6
Western, Arkansas	68.1	65.1	59,778	.81140	102.0
Central, Arkansas	96.8	88.3	271,936	5.69620	91.5
Southern Colorado, Colorado	56.0	87.2	91,181	.52360	53.6
Delmarva	110.7	168.9	7,250	.01490	94.7
Northwest, Florida	78.2	114.5	33,275	.23750	121.3
Central Savannah River, Georgia	122.5	83.4	70,626	.35090	88.2
Chittahoochee-Flint, Georgia	47.5	15.3	23,632	.14480	87.6
Coastal, Georgia	88.8	139.5	21,703	.35480	117.6
Georgia Mountains, Georgia	87.3	95.7	16,523	.10300	90.3
Coastal Plains, Georgia	82.3	139.6	30,652	.28520	100.2
Southwest, Georgia	81.9	126.6	55,890	.26330	98.1
Barren River, Kentucky	101.5	80.0	28,338	.19940	107.5
East Central, Michigan	88.0	70.8	179,648	.43060	89.7
East Central, Mississippi	79.5	44.5	49,374	.31250	88.4
Southern, Mississippi	85.7	85.4	17,155	.04100	67.7
Southwest, Mississippi	75.5	57.0	23,791	.15000	82.0
Bootheel, Missouri	64.0	32.3	13,765	.08060	50.3
New Hampshire-Vermont	70.7	44.1	12,294	.06210	70.6
Mohawk Valley, New York	57.7	67.2	150,558	.48350	52.2
Southeastern, North Carolina	166.1	54.2	47,106	.10060	96.6
Mid-East, North Carolina	88.1	49.6	22,860	.14860	108.2
Necese River, North Carolina	93.4	86.5	28,873	.08050	102.4
Ohio Valley, Ohio	85.5	54.2	24,957	.05990	62.1
N.E.C.O., Oklahoma	74.8	68.6	6,639	.04580	59.0
South Central, Oklahoma	51.6	84.5	20,009	.09500	72.2
S.O.D.A., Oklahoma	65.7	62.5	20,184	.13670	61.3
Upper Cumberland, Tennessee	115.7	61.9	7,805	.04450	92.5
Central, Texas	68.2	67.5	97,808	.32410	103.0
Coastal Bend, Texas	78.0	67.5	174,646	.45450	66.5
Six County, Utah	70.9	5.5	4,412	.13440	71.8
Cumberland Rateau, Virginia	80.5	27.5	4,963	.04030	74.7

Source: Office of Business Economics, U.S. Department of Commerce.

171

APPENDIX C

Despite significant technical limitations, Social Security Administration (SSA) data are well suited for regional labor force and migration analyses. The SSA maintains, on magnetic tape, an annual 1-percent sample of all Social Security records based on specific digits in a person's Social Security number. Because the same Social Security numbers are selected for inclusion each year, it is possible to establish a work-history file for all relevant persons who worked in a given period and to determine their socioeconomic characteristics for prior or subsequent years. (Before making the data available, all identification of individuals is removed by the SSA.) This file provides information on the demographic characteristics of workers, their wages, their industry, and their geographic location. Specifically the annual file brings together information from three sources: (1) data on sex, race, and date of birth are obtained from the employee's application for a Social Security number; (2) data on industry and county are obtained from the employer's application for an identification number; and (3) quarterly data on earnings are obtained from employers' contribution reports.

Although Social Security benefits and taxes have increased substantially in recent years, there have been no major changes in the coverage provisions of the Social Security system since 1954. The SSA sample covers almost 90 percent of persons in paid employment.

There are two types of SSA coverage: mandatory and elective. Employees in profit-making nonfarm industries, regular domestic employees, and
federal employees not covered by the federal retirement system are covered on a mandatory basis.
Groups covered on an elective basis, individually
or jointly, include ministers, employees in non-
profit establishments, and state and local government workers. Farm employees and household workers
who meet minimum earnings and length of employment
conditions are covered on a mandatory basis. Excluded from Social Security coverage are most federal civilian workers and railroad workers covered
under the Railroad Retirement Act. Data for regular self-employed are also available but were not
included in this study.

The SSA sample fills an important gap in regional data for employment, migration, earnings,
and work-force participation. It is important to
note that a considerable amount of data needed for
regional economic analysis are not readily available. Census data give information on net migration flows by county, but not on gross flows. Moreover only limited regional demographic data are
available, aside from those on employment, wages,
and migration for whites and Negroes, for males and
females, and for the young and old. Unlike the
Social Security sample, which is longitudinal, the
decennial censuses do not provide data for the same
workers over time. Instead they provide data for
workers in the same regional demographic category
at selected periods in time.

If a worker holds more than one job during the
year, his earnings from all jobs are combined in
the Social Security sample data in order to determine his total wages. However only one place of
work and one industry of employment are assigned to
each worker. For multiple jobholders, the industry
and geographic location of the employer paying the
highest wages are the determining factors in making
this assignment.

The problem of statistical sampling errors in
tabulations made from the 1-percent sample has been
examined in a number of documents. They indicate

that the 1-percent sample will yield reasonably re-
liable estimates of mobility, as long as the number
of workers in any tabulated group is not too small.
The SSA has suggested that it is reasonably safe to
treat the data as random. In the following table
the chances are 19 out of 20 that the sample value
will not differ from the true value by more than
the specified percentage variation:

Number of Workers in Sample	Percent Variation	Number of Workers in Sample	Percent Variation
5	87	1,000	6
10	63	2,500	4
50	28	5,000	3
100	20	10,000	2
500	9	50,000	1

Source: Values supplied by David Hirschberg,
Office of Business Economics.

In the table that follows, a migrant is defined as any person who worked in a survey area
county on April 1, 1965 but who worked in a SMSA in
a different county in 1970. The "estimated number
of migrants" values are the number of migrants in
the sample multiplied by 100. Only SMSAs receiving
at least two migrants from a survey area in the
sample are included. The SMSAs shown account for
77 percent of the total migration to SMSAs between
1965 and 1970.

The principal difficulty in comparing the migration flows shown below with the location preferences expressed in the surveys is that the 1-percent
sample picked up very few migrants under the age of
25 years in 1970. Of the 167 sample migrants shown
in the table, only 12 were in this category. It
must also be recognized that sampling errors are no
doubt high, because of the relatively small populations of the survey areas. Given these and other
limitations of the data, it is particularly difficult to make generalizations about eastern Kentucky
and southwest Mississippi, which had populations of

SMSA	Estimated Number of Migrants	Mean Wage, 1965	Mean Wage, 1970	Percent Change
Eastern Kentucky				
Huntington, West Virginia	1,000	5,840	8,399	43.8
Detroit, Michigan	400	322	847	163.0
Charleston, West Virginia	300	5,094	9,117	78.9
Louisville, Kentucky	200	7,308	5,978	-18.1
South Texas				
Houston, Texas	2,200	2,179	5,911	171.2
Corpus Christi, Texas	1,300	5,392	5,639	4.5
San Antonio, Texas	1,100	3,139	5,732	82.6
Austin, Texas	1,000	2,896	4,480	54.6
Dallas, Texas	800	2,174	6,314	190.4
McAllen, Texas	700	2,415	3,671	52.0
Brownsville, Texas	500	3,530	4,434	25.6
Los Angeles, California	500	2,028	7,036	246.9
Chicago, Illinois	400	3,006	5,647	87.8
Fort Worth, Texas	300	1,610	2,382	47.9
San Jose, California	300	1,533	5,764	275.9
Sioux City, Iowa	200	924	8,676	838.9
Tampa, Florida	200	4,134	7,400	79.0
Lansing, Michigan	200	1,254	5,128	308.9
Phoenix, Arizona	200	1,984	2,412	21.5
New Mexico-Arizona				
Albuquerque, New Mexico	1,200	3,575	4,559	27.5
Los Angeles, California	800	2,695	6,912	156.4
Phoenix, Arizona	500	4,615	5,575	20.8
Denver, Colorado	300	5,936	9,881	66.4
New York, New York	300	3,580	9,229	157.7
San Bernardino, California	300	3,028	4,725	56.0
Tucson, Arizona	300	5,632	5,886	4.5
Oklahoma City, Oklahoma	200	5,590	4,232	-24.2
San Francisco, California	200	2,274	2,476	8.8
Southwest Mississippi				
Birmingham, Alabama	600	2,826	3,728	31.9
New Orleans, Louisiana	200	2,394	6,358	165.5

134,307 and 67,314, respectively, in 1970. Perhaps
the most noteworthy phenomenon with respect to
these areas is the large number of persons migrating to intermediate-sized cities in a neighboring
state--to Huntington and Charleston, West Virginia
in the case of eastern Kentucky; to Birmingham,
Alabama in the case of southwest Mississippi.
Blacks account for 400 of the migrants to Birmingham and for 100 of those to New Orleans.

Migrants from south Texas, which had a 1970
population of 416,821, had a high propensity to go
to other Texan SMSAs. Houston was clearly the most
favored destination. Houston and Dallas both accounted for relatively high percentage income increases for migrants. However, the intermediate
cities--in terms of size and location--of Corpus
Christi, San Antonio, and Austin received more migrants in relation to their own size than did
Houston or Dallas. Although they received fewer
migrants than any of these Texan cities, Los Angeles
and San Jose both gave migrants high percentage increases in income.

Albuquerque attracted more New Mexican and
Arizonan migrants than any other SMSA, though the
highest percentage income increases were accounted
for by Los Angeles and New York. The relatively
nearby SMSAs of Phoenix, Denver, and Tucson also
attracted a large number of migrants.

CHAPTER 1

1. Niles M. Hansen, French Regional Planning (Bloomington: Indiana University Press, 1968); Rural Poverty and the Urban Crisis (Bloomington: Indiana University Press, 1970); Intermediate-Size Cities as Growth Centers (New York: Praeger Publishers, 1971).

2. Norman Beckman, "Development of National Urban Growth Policy," Journal of the American Institute of Planners, XXXVII, 3 (May 1971), 161.

3. Ibid., pp. 146-47. The act in question is United States Public Law 91-609.

4. Ibid., p. 152.

5. Ibid.

6. Commission on Population Growth and the American Future, Population Growth and America's Future (an interim report) (Washington, D.C., 1971), p. 47.

7. National Goals Research Staff, Toward Balanced Growth: Quantity with Quality (Washington, D.C., July 4, 1970), p. 223.

8. Ibid., pp. 46-47.

9. Ibid., p. 43.

10. Ibid., p. 28.

11. Ibid., p. 60.

12. William Alonso, "What Are New Towns For?" Urban Studies, VII, 1 (February 1970), 54.

13. Toward Balanced Growth, p. 57.

14. Ibid., p. 58.

15. Brian J. L. Berry, "Labor Market Participation and Regional Potential," Growth and Change, I, 4 (October 1970), 3.

16. Ibid., p. 10.

17. E. A. G. Robinson, ed., Backward Areas in Advanced Countries (New York: St. Martin's Press, 1969), p. xvi. Some scholars would argue that the 250,000 level may be an approximate minimum for an efficient growth center strategy; see Hansen, Rural Poverty and the Urban Crisis, pp. 249-51.

18. The Economic and Social Condition of Rural America in the 1970's, Economic Research Service, U.S. Department of Agriculture, for the Senate Committee on Government Operations, 92d Congress, 1st session (Washington, D.C., 1971), p. 33.

19. President's National Advisory Commission on Rural Poverty, The People Left Behind (Washington, D.C., 1967).

20. U.S. Department of Agriculture, Communities of Tomorrow, Agriculture 2000 (Washington, D.C., 1968).

21. Economic Development Administration, Regional Development in the United States, Part 2 (Washington, D.C., 1967), p. VI-41.

22. Vida Nichols, "Growth Poles: An Evaluation of Their Propulsive Effects," Environment and Planning, I, 2 (1969), 194.

23. François Perroux, "La notion de pôle de croissance," L'économie du XXème siècle (2d ed.; Paris: Presses Universitaires de France, 1964), p. 143. This article originally appeared in Economie appliquée, Nos. 1-2 (1955).

24. J. R. Boudeville, Problems of Regional Economic Planning (Edinburgh: University of Edinburgh Press, 1966), p. 112.

25. Albert O. Hirschman, The Strategy of Economic Development (New Haven: Yale University Press, 1958), pp. 183-201.

26. Ibid., p. 187. See also Gunnar Myrdal, Rich Lands and Poor (New York: Harper and Brothers, 1957), pp. 31-33, where the term "spread effects" was first coined.

27. For example, see Brian J. L. Berry, op. cit.; and "Spatial Organization and Levels of Welfare: Degree of Metropolitan Labor Market Participation as a Variable in Economic Development" (paper presented to the Economic Development Administration Research Conference, Washington, D.C., October 9-13, 1967).

28. Hansen French Regional Planning, pp. 117-18, 176-83.

29. Nichols, op. cit.

30. Lloyd D. Bender, Bernal L. Green, and Rex R. Campbell, "A Case Study: Trickle Down and Leakage in the War on Poverty," Growth and Change, II, 4 (October 1971), 40.

31. Ibid.

32. Irwin Gray, "Employment Effect of a New
Industry in a Rural Area," Monthly Labor Review,
XCII, 6 (June 1969), 29.

33. Appalachia, II, 9 (June-July 1969), 8.

34. Appalachia, IV, 6 (March-April 1971), 19.

35. Appalachia, II, 9 (June-July 1969), 1-10.

36. Ibid., p. 9. See also Appalachia, IV, 6
(March-April 1971), 5.

37. "Appalachia as a Developing Nation," Business Week (July 18, 1970), pp. 46-54.

38. Luther J. Carter, "Appalachian Program:
A Mechanism for a National Growth Policy," Science,
CLXIX, 3940 (July 3, 1970), 35.

39. Ben A. Franklin, "In Appalachia: Vast
Aid, Scant Relief," The New York Times, November 29,
1970, pp. 1, 56.

40. John Fetterman, "Absentee Asset," Louisville Courier-Journal Magazine (February 28, 1971),
p. 32.

41. Ibid., p. 33.

42. Charles K. Fairchild, Worker Relocation:
A Review of U.S. Department of Labor Mobility Demonstration Projects (Washington, D.C.: E. F. Shelley,
1970), p. 20.

CHAPTER 2

1. John Lansing and Eva Mueller, The Geographic Mobility of Labor (Ann Arbor, Mich.: University of Michigan Survey Research Center, 1967),
pp. 15-17.

2. "Mobility of the Population of the United
States: March, 1967 to March, 1968," Current Population Reports, Series P-20, No. 188, U.S. Bureau
of the Census (Washington, D.C., 1969).

3. Lansing and Mueller, op. cit., p. 59.

4. Peter A. Morrison, "Urban Growth, New
Cities, and the 'Population Problem'" (Santa Monica,
Cal.: Rand Corporation, unpublished paper, Decem-
ber 1970).

5. Varden Fuller, Rural Worker Adjustment to
Urban Life (Ann Arbor, Mich.: Institute of Labor
and Industrial Relations of the University of Michigan and Wayne State University, 1970), p. 47.

6. "Editorial Note," New Generation, L, 3
(Summer 1968), 1.

7. For a brief review, see Charles K. Fairchild, <u>Worker Relocation: A Review of U.S. Department of Labor Mobility Demonstration Projects</u> (Washington, D.C.: E. F. Shelley, 1970), pp. 23-26.

8. Unless otherwise indicated, the discussion of these forms of assistance is based on Organisation for Economic Cooperation and Development, <u>Government Financial Aid to Geographical Mobility in OECD Countries</u> (Paris: OECD, 1967).

9. Eli Ginzberg, "Sweden's Manpower Policies: A Look at the Leader," <u>Manpower</u>, II, 11 (November 1970), 26.

10. Martin Schnitzer, <u>Programs for Relocating Workers Used by Governments of Selected Countries</u>, Joint Economic Committee, 89th Congress, 2d session, Economic Policies and Practices Paper No. 8 (Washington, D.C., 1966), pp. 22-35.

11. <u>Ibid.</u>, p. 32. See also Sol Swerdloff, "Sweden's Manpower Programs," <u>Monthly Labor Review</u>, LXXXIX, 1 (January 1966), 1-2; and Carl G. Uhr, "Recent Swedish Labor Market Policies," in Garth L. Mangum, ed., <u>The Manpower Revolution</u> (Garden City, N.Y.: Doubleday Anchor Books, 1966), p. 377.

12. Ginzberg, <u>op. cit.</u>, p. 27.

13. Fairchild, <u>op. cit.</u>, pp. 2, 52.

14. <u>Ibid.</u>, p. 54.

15. <u>Ibid.</u>, pp. 57-59.

16. <u>Ibid.</u>

17. N. Dann Milne, "Toward an Improved Labor Relocation Program: Evaluating the Foreign and Domestic Experience," Discussion Paper No. 13 (Austin: University of Texas, Center for Economic Development, unpublished paper, October 1970), p. 48.

18. Fairchild, <u>op. cit.</u>, pp. 104-05.

19. <u>Ibid.</u>, pp. 5-6.

20. <u>Ibid.</u>, p. 78.

21. <u>Ibid.</u>, pp. 7-9, 142.

22. <u>Ibid.</u>, pp. 143-44.

23. Garth Mangum, "Moving Workers to Jobs: An Evaluation of the Labor Mobility Demonstration Program" (Washington, D.C.: Manpower Administration, U.S. Department of Labor, unpublished paper, 1969), p. 18.

24. Audrey Freedman, "Labor Mobility Projects for the Unemployed," Monthly Labor Review, XCI, 6 (June 1968), 62.

25. Fairchild, op. cit., p. 12.

26. Ibid., p. 111.

27. Ibid., p. 141.

28. This section is based entirely on an unpublished report on worker relocation prepared under the auspices of the U.S. Department of Labor by Beverly Bachemin, Bill Hood, and H. Pope Huff, all of whom have been creatively and effectively involved in pilot labor mobility projects. My firsthand investigations of projects in Kentucky, Mississippi, and Texas have influenced my choice of topics in this section.

CHAPTER 3

1. See, for example, Hansen, French Regional Planning, pp. 26-53.

2. See, for example, Commissariat Général du Plan, Rapport de la Commission nationale de l'aménagement du territoire pour l'orientation du VIe Plan (Paris, 1970), pp. 21, 27. 43.

3. For more detail on the institutional structure of French regional planning, see Hansen, op. cit.; and Intermediate-Size Cities as Growth Centers (New York: Praeger Publishers, 1971), pp. 42-47.

4. Henri Bastide and Alain Girard, "Les tendances démographiques en France et les attitudes de la population," Population, XXI, 1 (January-February 1966), 31.

5. Alain Girard and Henri Bastide, "Les problèmes démographiques devant l'opinion," Population, XV, 3 (April-May 1960), 287.

6. "La Région de Paris: perspectives de développement et d'aménagement," Sondages, No. 4 (1963), p. 26.

7. Hansen, French Regional Planning, pp. 36-37.

8. Bastide and Girard, op. cit., p. 33.

9. Ibid.

10. Le Monde, Sélection hebdomadaire, September 12-18, 1968, p. 9.

11.   Commissariat Général du Plan, op. cit.,
p. 20.

12.   "The Chicanos Campaign for a Better Deal,"
Business Week, No. 2177 (May 29, 1971), pp. 48-49.

13.   Leo Grebler, Joan W. Moore, and Ralph
Guzman, The Mexican-American People (New York: The
Free Press, 1970), pp. 185-87.

14.   Ibid., pp. 235-36.

15.   Ibid., pp. 206-07.   For other data on the
relatively poor situation of south Texas, see Fred
H. Schmidt, Spanish Surnamed American Employment in
the Southwest (Washington, D.C.:   U.S. Government
Printing Office, 1970); and Niles M. Hansen, Rural
Poverty and the Urban Crisis (Bloomington: Indiana
University Press, 1970), pp. 193-221.

16.   Quoted in Harold E. Fey and D'Arcy McNickle,
Indians and Other Americans (rev. ed.; New York:
Harper & Row, 1970), p. ix.   For details on economic
conditions prevalent on reservations see Helen W.
Johnson, Rural Indian Americans in Poverty, U.S. De-
partment of Agriculture Economic Research Service,
Agricultural Economic Report No. 167 (Washington,
D.C., 1969); and Alan L. Sorkin, American Indians
and Federal Aid (Washington, D.C.:   The Brookings
Institution, 1971).

17.   See William A. Brophy and Sophie D.
Aberle, The Indian: America's Unfinished Business
(Norman: University of Oklahoma Press, 1966).

18.   Stuart Levine and Nancy O. Lurie, eds.,
The American Indian Today (Baltimore: Penguin
Books, 1970), p. 26.

19.   Vine Deloria Jr., Custer Died for Your
Sins (New York: Macmillan, 1969), p. 131.

20.   Ibid., p. 142.   See also Stan Steiner,
The New Indians (New York: Delta, 1968), p. 134.

21.   "Role of Manpower Programs in Assisting
the American Indians," in Joint Economic Committee,
Toward Economic Development for Native American
Communities, Vol. 1, Part I, Development Prospects
and Problems (Washington, D.C., 1969), pp. 141-42.
See also Fey and McNickle, op. cit., p. 244.

22.   Sorkin, op. cit., p. 81.

23.   Ibid., p. 215.

24.   Ibid., pp. 215-16.

25. In 1970 the Albuquerque SMSA had a population of 313,829, an increase of 19.7 percent over
the 1960 population; U.S. Bureau of the Census, Population of Standard Metropolitan Statistical Areas,
Preliminary Reports, 1970 Census of Population,
PC(P3)-3, United States.

26. U.S. Bureau of the Census, City and County
Data Book, 1967 (Washington, D.C., 1967), pp. 192-202.

CHAPTER 4

1. See A Study of Economic Consequences of
Rural to Urban Migration, Tracor Incorporated Project 235-006 (OEO Contract B89-4594), December 1969.
See also Niles M. Hansen, Intermediate-Size Cities
as Growth Centers (New York: Praeger Publishers,
1971), pp. 149-80.

2. George P. Huber and Joseph C. Ullman, "Computer Job Matching--How and How Well," Manpower, II,
11 (November 1970), 6.

3. See Joe M. Bohlen and Ray E. Wakeley, "In-
tentions to Migrate and Actual Migration of Rural
High School Graduates," Rural Sociology, XV, 4 (December 1950), 328-34.

CHAPTER 5

1. Sar A. Levitan, Federal Aid to Depressed
Areas (Baltimore: The Johns Hopkins Press, 1964).

2. United States Public Law 89-4, Appalachian
Regional Development Act of 1965, 89th Congress,
Sec. 224 (a); and United States Public Law 89-136,
Public Works and Economic Development Act of 1965,
89th Congress, Sec. 502.

3. Appalachian Regional Commission, State and
Regional Development Plans, 1968 (Washington, D.C.,
1968).

4. The values are based on the average annual
increase from 1947 to 1965; Economic Report of the
President, 1967 (Washington, D.C., 1967), p. 83.

5. Edwin C. Harper, "The Appalachian Experiment: Regional Commissions Pro and Con," Appalachia,
III, 10 (August 1970), 13.

CHAPTER 6

1. Unless otherwise indicated, the data in this chapter are taken from Economic Research Service, U.S. Department of Agriculture, The Economic and Social Condition of Rural America in the 1970's, Part 1 (Washington, D.C., 1971), which was prepared for the Senate Committee on Government Operations, 92d Congress, 1st session.

2. Ibid., p. 50.

3. Vernon Briggs, "Chicanos and Rural Poverty: A Continuing Issue for the 1970's" (unpublished paper prepared for the Center for the Study of Human Resources, University of Texas, May 1971), p. 40.

4. George Iden, "Unemployment Classification of Major Labor Areas, 1950-65," Journal of Human Resources, II, 3 (Summer 1967), 391.

5. Gene Laber, "Unemployment Classification of Major Labor Areas, 1950-65: A Comment," Journal of Human Resources, III, 4 (Fall 1968), 515-19.

6. Lloyd D. Bender, Bernal L. Green, and Rex R. Campbell, "Trickle-down and Leakage in the War on Poverty," Growth and Change, II, 4 (October 1971), 40. See also Irwin Gray, "Employment Effect of a New Industry in a Rural Area," Monthly Labor Review, XCII, 6 (June 1969), 29.

7. Ibid.

8. Wilbur R. Thompson, "The Economic Base of Urban Problems," in Neil W. Chamberlain, ed., Contemporary Economic Issues (Homewood, Ill.: Richard D. Irwin, 1969), p. 8.

9. For an extended treatment of growth-center theory and policy, see Hansen, Intermediate-Size Cities as Growth Centers; and Niles M. Hansen, ed., Growth Centers and Regional Development (New York: The Free Press, 1972).

10. Alexander Ganz, "Our Large Cities: New Directions and New Approaches" (M.I.T., Cambridge, Mass.: A Summary of Findings, M.I.T. Laboratory for Environmental Studies, mimeo., December 3, 1969), p. 25.

11. Ibid., p. 25.

12. William Alonso, "The Question of City Size and National Policy" (University of California, Berkeley, Center for Planning and Development Research, Working Paper No. 125, unpublished manuscript, June 1970), p. 2.

13. Ibid., p. 5.

14. Ibid., p. 7.

15. Brian J. L. Berry, "Labor Market Participation and Regional Potential," Growth and Change, I, 4 (October 1970), 10.

16. Wilbur R. Thompson, "The Economic Base of Urban Problems," in Neil W. Chamberlain, ed., Contemporary Economic Issues (Homewood, Ill.: Richard D. Irwin, 1969), p. 11. The emphasis is Thompson's.

17. "For Executives, Fun City Can Be a Hardship," Business Week, February 7, 1970, p. 64. See also Wall Street Journal, March 24, 1969, p. 1; and Time, April 26, 1971, pp. 86-87.

18. Wilbur R. Thompson, "The National System of Cities as an Object of Public Policy," Urban Studies, IX, 1 (February 1972), 108.

19. Ibid., p. 24.

20. Varden Fuller, Rural Worker Adjustment to Urban Life (Ann Arbor, Mich.: University of Michigan and Wayne State University Institute of Labor and Industrial Relations, 1970), p. 7.

21. John Friedmann and John Miller, "The Urban Field," Journal of the American Institute of Planners, XXXI, 4 (November 1965); reprinted in Brian J. L. Berry and Frank E. Horton, Geographic Perspectives on Urban Systems (Englewood Cliffs, N.J.: Prentice Hall, 1970), p. 56. See also J. R. Lasuen, "On Growth Poles," Urban Studies, VI, 2 (June 1969), 137-61; and Berry, op. cit.

22. Friedmann and Miller, op. cit., p. 56.

23. John A. Kuehn and Jerry G. West, "Highways and Regional Development," Growth and Change, II, 3 (July 1971), 27.

24. See, for example, George W. Wilson, et al., The Impact of Highway Investment on Development (Washington, D.C.: The Brookings Institution, 1966); John M. Munro, "Planning the Appalachian Development Highway System: Some Critical Questions," Land Economics, XLV, 2 (May 1969), 149; and Benjamin Higgins, "Regional Disparities and National Welfare" (York University Harris and Partners Lecture Series, unpublished manuscript, March 1970), p. 16; and Dick Netzer, Economics and Urban Problems (New York: Basic Books, 1970), pp. 148-49.

25. Glenn V. Fuguitt, "The Places Left Behind: Population Trends and Policy for Rural America," Rural Sociology, XXXVI, 4 (December 1971), 449-70.

26. Ibid., pp. 456-58.

27. Ibid., p. 462.

28. Ibid., p. 466.

29. Alfred S. Eichner, State Development Agencies and Employment Expansion (Ann Arbor, Mich.: University of Michigan and Wayne State University Institute of Labor and Industrial Relations, 1970), p. 2.

30. South Carolina provides a particularly good example of coordinated programs to match job training with the labor needs of new industry. See Eichner, op. cit., pp. vi, 31, 43-44, 62-65.

31. Thompson, "The Economic Base," pp. 25-26. See also Wilbur R. Maki, "Infrastructure in Rural Areas," in President's National Advisory Committee on Rural Poverty, Rural Poverty in the United States (Washington, D.C., 1968), pp. 86-109.

32. For other supporting evidence see Robert J. Saunders, "Population Flows, Spatial Economic Activity and Urban Areas in Appalachia," The Annals of Regional Science, V, 1 (June 1971), 125-36.

NILES M. HANSEN is Professor of Economics and Director, Center for Economic Development, at the University of Texas. He is the author of <u>French Regional Planning</u>, <u>France in the Modern World</u>, <u>Rural Poverty and the Urban Crisis</u>, <u>Intermediate-Size Cities as Growth Centers</u>, and the editor of <u>Growth Centers in Regional Economic Development</u>. He also has contributed numerous articles to professional journals in economics and the social sciences. Professor Hansen is a member of the Board of Editors of <u>Growth and Change</u>, <u>Review of Regional Studies</u>, and <u>Regional and Urban Economics</u>.

Professor Hansen received his doctoral degree from Indiana University.